Pope Francis

MORNING HOMILIES II

Pope Francis

MORNING HOMILIES II

In the Chapel of St. Martha's Guest House
September 2, 2013 – January 31, 2014

Translated by Dinah Livingstone

ORBIS BOOKS
Maryknoll, New York 10545

Founded in 1970, Orbis Books endeavors to publish works that enlighten the mind, nourish the spirit, and challenge the conscience. The publishing arm of the Maryknoll Fathers and Brothers, Orbis seeks to explore the global dimensions of the Christian faith and mission, to invite dialogue with diverse cultures and religious traditions, and to serve the cause of reconciliation and peace. The books published reflect the views of their authors and do not represent the official position of the Maryknoll Society. To learn more about Maryknoll and Orbis Books, please visit our website at www.maryknollsociety.org.

Library of Congress Cataloging-in-Publication Data

Francis, Pope, 1936-
[Sermons. Selections. English]
Pope Francis morning homilies : in the Chapel of St. Martha's guest house / translated by Dinah Livingstone.
3 volumes cm
Contents: [1] 22 March-6 July 2013—II. September 2, 2013-January 31, 2014
ISBN 978-1-62698-111-9 (v. 1 : pbk.)—ISBN 978-1-62698-147-8 (v.
1. Catholic Church—Sermons. I. Title.
  BX1756.F677S4713 2015
  252'.02—dc23
  2014033307

Contents

v

Preface

✄

Each morning Pope Francis begins his day by celebrating Mass in the chapel of St. Martha's Guest House, where he has chosen to live. Those in attendance vary, including other residents and staff of the Guest House, curial officials, visiting dignitaries, foreign bishops, representatives of religious congregations, or others who manage day-to-day life in the Vatican State, such as the gardening and waste collection staff. This volume of the Pope's *Morning Homilies*, the second in an ongoing series, is again based on the accounts published each day in *L'Osservatore Romano*. Through these accounts it is possible for those not present to experience and enjoy the Pope's lively manner of speaking and his capacity to engage his listeners and their daily lives.

We know what great significance Pope Francis attaches to preaching. In his apostolic exhortation *Evangelii Gaudium* he has dedicated an entire chapter to the homily, *the touchstone for judging a pastor's closeness and ability to communicate to his people* (EG 125). There he provides numerous guidelines for effective preaching, noting that the homily *should be brief and avoid taking on the semblance of a speech or a lecture*; it should be positive, *not so much concerned with pointing out what shouldn't be done, but with suggesting what we can do better*; it should respect the original intent of the text (*if a text was written to console, it should not be used to correct errors*); it should avoid *abstract truths and cold syllogisms;* and it should make effective use of imagery (here he reinforces his point by recalling the words of an old teacher, who taught him that a good homily should have *an idea, a sentiment, an image*). Above all, he likens the homily to a conversation "between a mother and child": *Even if the homily at times may be somewhat tedious, if this maternal and ecclesial spirit is present, it will always bear fruit, just as the tedious counsels of a mother bear fruit, in due time, in the hearts of her children* (140).

From his morning homilies at St. Martha's we can see how closely Pope Francis heeds his own advice. His homilies are certainly short and positive, filled with memorable images (thus, he speaks of a *holiness from the dry cleaners, meaning everything fine and dandy, and everything done well, but without the fervor that pushes us to preach the Lord*). They are marked by his familiar themes: the importance of mercy and forgiveness, the role of Jesus as Savior, the dangers of a church closed in on itself, the gospel as a source of life and joy.

But what is most striking is the intimacy and spontaneity of these homilies. Here is not the voice of a pontiff addressing the cares of the world, the universal church, or even the church of Rome, but a pastor sharing the Word of God with his immediate flock. He directs the message as much to himself as anyone else, acknowledging the same challenges, seeking the same consolation and healing.

The homily, as Pope Francis has observed, can be *an intense and happy experience of the Spirit, a consoling encounter with God's word, a constant source of renewal and growth* (EG, 135). May that happy experience become available to all who read this book!

—*Robert Ellsberg*

Pope Francis

MORNING HOMILIES

In the Chapel of St. Martha's Guest House

THE DANGER OF GOSSIP

Monday, September 2, 2013
LK 4:16-30

The tongue, gossip, and backbiting are weapons that undermine the community every day; they incite envy, jealousy, and lust for power. You can kill someone that way. For speaking of peace also means thinking about how much harm it's possible to do with your tongue. This was the serious point of Pope Francis' homily at the Mass celebrated in the chapel of St. Martha's Guest House, a daily custom which he resumed this morning of Monday, September 2.

The pope drew his inspiration from the story of Jesus' return to Nazareth, as told in Luke (4:16-30), one of the most "dramatic" gospel passages in which, said the pope, "we can see what our souls are like" and how the wind can blow them this way and that. In Nazareth, the pope explained, "they were all waiting for Jesus. Everyone wanted to meet him. He came to meet his own people. For the first time he returned to his home town. They were waiting because they had heard about all the things he'd done in Capernaum, his miracles. When the service began, as usual, they invited the guest to read from the book. Jesus did so and read from the prophet Isaiah, a sort of prophecy about himself, and that was why he concluded his reading by saying: 'Today this scripture you have just heard has been fulfilled.'"

Their first reaction was fine, explained the pope. They were all delighted. But then a slither of envy wormed its way into someone's mind and he began to say: "But where did this guy study? Isn't he Joseph's son? We know all his family. What university did he go to?" And they began demanding him to do a miracle: only then would they believe. "They wanted a show," the pope said: "'Do a miracle and we'll believe in you.' But Jesus isn't a showman."

Jesus did no miracles in Nazareth. Thus he pointed to the lack of faith of those asking for a "show." "These people," said Pope Francis, "were so angry that they got up and pushed Jesus to the top of a mountain to throw him down and kill him." What had started happily threatened to end in crime, the murder of Jesus "out of envy and jealousy." But we're not talking only about something that happened two thousand years ago, the bishop of Rome made clear. "This happens every day," he said, "in our hearts, in our communities," every time we welcome someone by speaking well of them on the first day and then less and less well until it turns into gossip that almost "flays them alive." Anyone who gossips in a community about a brother or sister ends up "wanting to kill them," the pope stressed. "The apostle John," he recalled, "tells us in his first letter, chapter 3 verse 15: anyone who hates his brother in his heart is a murderer." And immediately the pope went on to say: "We're accustomed to backbiting and gossip," and we often turn our communities and even our family into a "hell," where this kind of wrong leads us to "kill our brother and sister by our tongue."

"The Bible," continued the pope, "says that the devil came into the world through envy. A community, a family, can be destroyed by this envy the devil puts into our hearts, making us speak ill of others." And referring to what happens today, he stressed that we need to think about our daily weapons: "the tongue, backbiting, gossip."

So, the pope asked, how can we build a community? And his reply was: "As it is in heaven," as God's word proclaims: "The voice of the archangel is heard, the sound of God's trumpet, the day of resurrection. And after that it says: Thus we shall be with the Lord forever." So "for there to be peace in a community, a family, a country, in the world, we must begin being with the Lord. For where the Lord is, there's no envy, no wrong, no jealousy. There's kindness. Let us ask this from the Lord: never to kill our neighbor by our tongue and to be with the Lord as we all shall be in heaven."

A Gentle, Modest Light, Full of Love

Tuesday, September 3, 2013
1 Thes 5:1-6, 9-11; Luke 4:31-37

Humility, gentleness, love, the experience of the cross, are the means by which the Lord defeats evil. And the light Jesus brought into the world heals human blindness, often dazzled by the world's false, strong but deceiving light. It is up to us to discern which light comes from God. This was the theme of Pope Francis' reflection during the Mass celebrated this morning, Tuesday, September 3, in the chapel of St. Martha's Guest House.

Commenting on the first reading, the Holy Father focused on the "beautiful words" Paul writes to the Thessalonians: "But you, beloved, are all children of light and children of day, not children of night. We do not belong to night or to darkness" (1 Thessalonians 5:1-6, 9-11). It's clear, explained the pope, what the apostle is trying to say: "Being Christian means belonging to light, not to darkness." Jesus brought this light into the world. "In the first chapter of his gospel," continued the pope, "St. John tells us 'the light came into the world,' the light that is Jesus." A light that "was not well received by the world" but which still "saves us from darkness, the darkness of sin."

Today, the pope continued, people think it's possible to get this light, which dispels the darkness, by means of so many scientific discoveries and other human inventions, through which "we can know everything, we can have knowledge of everything." But "the light of Jesus," the pope declared, "is something else. It isn't the light of ignorance, no, no! It's a light of knowledge, a light of wisdom. But it's also something else. The light the world offers us is artificial. It may be bright, even brighter than the light of Jesus, eh? Bright as a firework, a camera flash. Whereas the light of Jesus is a gentle light, a calm light, a peaceful light. It's like the light of Christmas Eve: unpretentious. It's like that: beaming and giving peace. The light of Jesus isn't spectacular: it's a light that shines into our hearts. It's true, as St. Paul tells us, that often the devil comes disguised as an angel of light. He likes to imitate the light of Jesus. He pretends to be good and speaks to us like that, calmly, as he did to Jesus when he'd been fasting in the wilderness: 'If you're the son of God, do this miracle, throw yourself down from the temple,' do something spectacular! And he says this calmly," which is how he deceives.

So Pope Francis recommended that we should "ask the Lord for the wisdom of discernment to recognize when it is Jesus giving us light and when it is the devil disguised as an angel of light. How many people believe they are living in the light but are in darkness and don't know it!"

But what is the light that Jesus offers us? "We can recognize it," the Holy Father explained, "because it's a modest light. It isn't an imposing light, but modest. It's a gentle light, with the power of gentleness; it's a light that speaks to our hearts and also a light that offers the cross. If we in our inner light are gentle, we hear Jesus' voice in our hearts and look fearlessly at the cross in Jesus' light." But if, on the other hand, we let ourselves be dazzled by a light that makes us feel secure and proud, makes us look down on others, scorn them haughtily, then we're certainly not in the presence of the "light of Jesus." Instead it's the "light of the devil disguised as Jesus," said the bishop of Rome, "disguised as an angel of light. We must always make the distinction: where Jesus is, there's always humility, gentleness, love, and the cross. We'll never find Jesus without humility, without gentleness, without love, and without the cross. He walked that way of light before us. We must walk behind him without fear," because "Jesus has the strength and authority to give us that light." A strength described in the gospel passage for today's liturgy, in which Luke tells the story, set in Capernaum, of the casting out of the devil from the man possessed (cf. Luke 4:16-39). "The people were awestruck," commented the pope on the reading, "they were full of fear and, says the gospel, they asked one another: 'What word is this that commands impure spirits with authority and power and they depart?' Jesus doesn't need an army to chase off demons, he doesn't need pride, he doesn't need strength, or arrogance." What is this word "that commands impure spirits with authority and power and they depart?" asked the pope. "It's a word," he replied, "that is humble, gentle, very loving." It's a word that's with us in moments of suffering that brings us close to the cross of Jesus. "Let us ask the Lord," Pope Francis concluded, "to give us the grace of his light today and to teach us to distinguish between his light and the artificial light created by the enemy to deceive us."

Listening, Renunciation, and Mission

Thursday, September 5, 2013
Lk 5:1-11; Col 1:9-14[4]

When the Lord passes by in our lives, he always says a word to us and makes us a promise. But he also asks us to give up something and entrusts us with a mission. Pope Francis recalled this during the Mass celebrated this morning, Thursday, September 5, in the chapel of St. Martha's Guest House.

Commenting on the story of the "miraculous draft of fishes," told by Luke (5:1-11) in the gospel passage read during the liturgy, the pope remembered St. Augustine, who constantly "repeats a sentence which has always struck me. He says: 'I'm afraid when the Lord passes by.' Why? 'Because I'm afraid he will pass by and I won't realize it.' And the Lord passes by in our lives, just as he does here in the lives of Peter, James, and John."

In this instance the Lord passed by in the lives of his disciples by doing a miracle. But, the pope pointed out, "Jesus doesn't always pass by in our lives with a miracle." Even though he always makes himself felt, he added. "Always. And when the Lord passes by, something always happens, like what happened here: he tells us something, makes us feel something, then he says a word to us which is a promise. He asks something from us in our way of life: to give something, to let something go. And then he gives us a mission."

These three aspects of Jesus' passing through our lives—telling us "a word which is a promise," asking us "to give up something," and entrusting us "with a mission"—appear clearly in this passage from Luke's gospel. The Holy Father stressed particularly Peter's reaction to Jesus' miracle: "Simon, who was so passionate, went up to Jesus and said: 'Depart from me, Lord, for I am a sinful man.' He really felt this because he was like that. And what does Jesus say to him? 'Don't be afraid.'"

"Such a beautiful word, so often repeated: 'Don't be afraid, fear not,'" commented the pope and added: "And then, and here's the promise he says to Peter: 'I will make you a fisher of men.' Whenever the Lord comes into our lives, when he passes by in our hearts, he says a word to us and gives us a promise: 'Go ahead, courage, don't be afraid: you will do this!'" It's "an invitation to follow him." And "when we hear this invitation and realize that there's something wrong about our lives, we must put it right," and we must be ready to leave anything, with generosity. Even if "there's something good in our lives," the pope continued, "Jesus invites us to leave it and follow him more closely. That's what happened to the apostles, who left everything, as the gospel says: 'And when they had landed the boats, they left everything and followed him.'"

So Christian life is "always following the Lord." But in order to follow him, we must first "hear what he's telling us"; and then "leave what at that moment we have to leave and follow him."

Finally, there's the mission with which Jesus entrusts us. In fact, "he never says: 'Follow me!' without then telling us our mission. He always says: 'Leave and follow me for this.'" So if "we walk along Jesus' road," the pope declared, "it's in order to do something. That's the mission."

It's "a sequence that's repeated even when we go to pray." In fact "our prayers," stressed the Holy Father, "must always have these three moments." First of all, listening to the word of Jesus, a word by which he gives us peace and assures us he is near. Then the moment of our renunciation: we must be ready to "leave something: 'Lord, what do you want me to leave in order to be closer to you?' Perhaps he doesn't say at that moment. But we must ask with generosity." Finally, the moment of mission: prayer always helps us to understand what "we have to do."

So that sums up our prayer: "Hearing the Lord, having the courage to give up something and finally to undertake a mission."

That doesn't mean we won't have to face temptations. Peter, re-called Pope Francis, sinned gravely when he denied Jesus. But then the Lord forgave him. James and John sinned by careerism. But the Lord forgave them too. So it's important to pray while keeping these three moments in mind. "We can ask the apostles, who lived so close to the Lord," he concluded, "for these things: to give us the grace always to pray listening to what Jesus says and to his promise; to make us willing to leave what prevents us from following Jesus closely; and to open our hearts to receive his mission."

THE GRACE OF JOY

Friday, September 6, 2013
LK 5:33-39; COL 1:15-20

Being a Christian means having the joy of belonging wholly to Christ, "the church's only bridegroom," and going to meet him as if you were going to a wedding. So joy and realizing that Christ is the center of our lives are the two attitudes that Christians should have day by day. Pope Francis reminded us of this in his homily during the Mass celebrated this morning, Friday, September 6, in the chapel of St. Martha's Guest House.

Pope Francis took his inspiration from the gospel passage read during the liturgy, in which Luke the evangelist describes the clash between Jesus and the scribes and Pharisees, because the disciples who are with him eat and drink while others are fast-ing (Luke 5:33-39). The pope explained what Jesus wanted to be understood in his reply to the scribes. He presents himself as the bridegroom: "He is the bridegroom. The church is the bride. And this image often recurs in the gospel," continued the pope.

"The wise virgins who wait for the bridegroom with their lamps lit; the feast the father gives for his son's marriage." In his reply to the scribes, said the pope, "the Lord says that when you're the bridegroom you can't fast, you can't be sad. He makes us see the relationship between himself and the church as a wedding." That is why, he explained, "the church cares so much for the sacrament of marriage. She calls it a great sacrament because it's the image of the union between Christ and the church." So when we speak of a wedding, "we're talking about a feast, we're talking about joy and this suggests the attitude we Christians should have": when we find Jesus Christ and begin to live according to the gospel, we Christians should do so joyfully. With joy, "because it's a great feast."

The Christian is fundamentally joyful. To bring home the image, the pope recalled the story of Jesus' miracle at the wedding at Cana. "If there's no wine there's no feast. Imagine," he said, "ending up drinking tea or fruit juice at that wedding...! That wouldn't do. So Mary asks for a miracle." That's what Christian life is like. It has this "joyful attitude, heartfelt joy."

Naturally, added the pope, "there are moments of the cross, moments of sorrow, but there's always that sense of deep peace. Why? Christian life is a feast, like the wedding of Jesus with the church." And here the Holy Father recalled how the first Christian martyrs went to their martyrdom as if they were going to a wedding; even at that moment their hearts were joyful. So the first attitude of the Christian who meets Jesus, repeated the pope, is like the church joining Jesus as his bride. "And at the end of the world," he added, there'll be the final feast, when the new Jerusalem will be dressed as a bride."

To explain the second attitude the Holy Father recalled the parable of the king's son's wedding (Matthew 22:1-14; Luke 14:16-24). "Some people," he recalled, "were so busy with their own affairs that they couldn't go to the feast. And the Lord, the

king, said: go out to the highways and byways and bring in everyone, travelers, the poor, the sick, the lepers and sinners, bring
them all in. Good and bad. They're all invited to the feast. And
the feast began. But then the king saw one man who wasn't wearing a wedding garment. Of course, we may well ask. 'But Father:
they were taken from the streets and then they are asked about
wedding garments? How come?' It's very simple: God asks us
for just one thing to go the feast: everything." Pope Francis explained: "The bridegroom's the most important, the bridegroom
fills everything. And that brings us to the first reading (Colossians 1:15-20), which speaks eloquently to us about Jesus being
all in all. Firstborn of all creation. In him all things were created
and they were created through him and for him; because he is the
center of all things. He is also the head of the body, the church.
He is the beginning. God has given him fullness, totality, to rec-
oncile all things in him."

This image makes us understand, continued the Holy Father,
that he is "everything," he is "the one and only"; he is "the only
bridegroom." And so if the Christian's first attitude "is feasting,
the second attitude is to recognize him as the only one. And anyone who doesn't recognize him hasn't got the right clothes to
go to the feast, to go to the wedding." If Jesus asks us for this
recognition it's because he as the bridegroom "is faithful, always
faithful. And he asks us to be faithful too." We cannot serve two
masters: "We either serve the Lord," said the pope, "or we serve
the world."

So this is "the second Christian attitude: to recognize Christ
as the all, the center, the fullness," even though there will always
be the temptation for us to reject this "newness of the gospel,
this new wine." So we have to welcome the newness of the gospel. Also because "old wineskins can't hold new wine." Jesus is
the church's bridegroom. He loves the church and gives his life
for her. He organizes a big wedding "feast. Jesus," concluded the

bishop of Rome, "demands a feast of joy. The joy of being Christians." He also asks us to be his alone. But if we behave or do things that don't go with being only his, "never mind: let us repent, let us ask for forgiveness and carry on," tirelessly "asking for the grace to be joyful."

No Christian without Jesus

Saturday, September 7, 2013
Col 1:21-23; Lk 6:1-5

There is no Christian without Jesus. And Jesus isn't there when the Christian answers to commands that don't lead to Jesus or don't come from Jesus. During the Mass celebrated this morning, Saturday, September 7, in St. Martha's Guest House, Pope Francis stressed that Christ is central. And he warned Christians against following private revelations, since, he said, revelation concluded with Christ.

In his homily this morning the Holy Father continued his reflection from yesterday, Friday, September 6, on readings in which Jesus was presented as the church's bridegroom. In today's gospel passage, taken from Luke (6:1-5), we hear the story of Jesus' discussion with the Pharisees, who reprimanded the apostles for breaking the Sabbath rest by picking and eating ears of wheat.

In this gospel passage, noted the pope, Jesus presents himself as something more than we had yesterday, "and he says: I am the Lord, also Lord of the Sabbath. In another place he says: The Sabbath was made for human beings, not human beings for the Sabbath. His own and the Christian's centrality in so many things. Jesus is the center, he is the Lord." A definition, said the pope, that "we don't understand well," because "it isn't easy to understand." What is certain is that Jesus "is the Lord;" it is he who "has the power, the glory, he who has the victory. He is the only Lord."

Quoting Paul's letter to the Colossians (1:21-23), the Holy Father noted the apostle tells us that Jesus "has reconciled us in his fleshly body through death—reconciled us all—to present you holy and blameless and irreproachable before him; provided that you continue securely established and steadfast in the faith." Jesus, said the pope, is the center who regenerates us and establishes us in the faith, whereas "the Pharisees put so many commandments at the center of their religiosity. And Jesus said of them: they place burdens on people's shoulders."

If Jesus is not at the center, continued the pope "other things are." And today "we find so many Christians without Christ, without Jesus. For example those who have the Pharisees' disease and are Christians who express their faith, their religiosity, their Christianity, in so many commandments: Oh, I've got to do this, I've got to do that. Duty Christians," that is to say, they do things because they have to do them but really "they don't know why they're doing them."

But "where is Jesus?" asked Pope Francis and continued: "A commandment is valid if it comes from Jesus." There are so many Christians without Christ, like those who "only go in for devotions, so many devotions, but Jesus isn't there. So then you're missing something, brother! You're missing Jesus. If your devotions lead you to Jesus, then fine. But if you just stay where you are, then something isn't right."

Then, he went on, "there's another group of Christians without Christ: those who seek out things that are a bit peculiar, a bit special, who go after private revelations," whereas revelation concluded with the new Testament. The Holy Father warned against those Christians who want "revelation as a spectacle, to hear something new." But Pope Francis urged, "take the gospel!" Lastly, the pope mentioned among Christians without Christ "those who sweeten their souls but lack virtue because they don't have Jesus."

So what is the rule for being a Christian with Christ? And what is the "sign" that someone is a Christian with Christ? "There's one very simple rule," the pope explained: only what brings you to Jesus is valid, and only what comes from Jesus is valid. Jesus is the center, the Lord, as he himself says."

So if something leads to or comes from Jesus, "go ahead," said the pope. But if it doesn't come from or lead to Jesus "then it's rather dangerous." And about the "sign" he said: "It's a simple sign, that of the man born blind, who comes in chapter nine of John's gospel. The gospel says that he prostrated himself before Jesus to worship him. A man or woman who worships Jesus is a Christian with Jesus. But if you can't worship Jesus, then something's missing in you."

So here's "a rule and a sign," concluded the pope. "The rule is this," he said. "I'm a good Christian, I'm on the right road to being a good Christian, if I do what comes from Jesus or what leads me to Jesus, because he's the center. The sign is worshiping Jesus, worshiping Jesus in prayer."

Jesus Is Hope

Monday, September 9, 2013
Col 1:24–2:3; Lk 6:6-11

It is sad to see those priests who have lost hope. That is why at the Mass celebrated this morning, Monday, September 9, in St. Martha's Guest House, Pope Francis invited the priests who were present to cultivate this virtue, "which for Christians has the name of Jesus." He said, "I see so many priests here today, so I want to tell you something: it's rather sad when you find a priest without hope, without that passion that rouses hope; and it's lovely when you find a priest coming to the end of his life who still has hope, not optimism but hope, who spreads hope." Because it means, he added, that "this priest is attached to Jesus Christ. And the people of God need us priests to give them hope in Jesus, who re-creates everything, and can re-create everything and is re-creating everything: in every Eucharist he re-creates creation, in every act of kindness he re-creates his love in us."

The pope spoke about hope, linking his reflection today to that of the days before, during which he had spoken of Jesus as the fullness, the center of Christian life, the church's only bridegroom. So today he focused on the idea expressed in St. Paul's letter to the Colossians (1:24–2:3): Jesus as "mystery, hidden mystery, God." God's mystery, which "appeared in Jesus," who is "our hope: he is our all, our center and also our hope."

Unfortunately, however, observed the bishop of Rome, "hope is a virtue" that's usually considered to be "second class. We don't believe that much in hope: we speak of faith and charity, but hope, as a French writer said, is a humble sort of virtue and we don't understand it very well."

Optimism, he explained, is a human attitude that depends on so many things; but hope is something else: "It's a gift, a present from the Holy Spirit, and that's why Paul tells us that it never disappoints us." And it also has a name. And "that name is Jesus"; we can't say we have hope in life if we don't hope in Jesus. "In that case it wouldn't be hope," he explained, "but good humor, optimism, like those sunny, positive people who always see the glass as half full rather than half empty."

The pope saw a confirmation of this idea in the passage from

Luke's gospel (6:6-11), referring to the theme of freedom. Luke's story presents us with a double slavery: that of the man "with the paralyzed hand who was a slave to his disability" and that "of the Pharisees and scribes who were slaves to their rigid, legalistic attitudes." Jesus "frees both: he shows those who are rigid that that isn't the way to freedom and he frees the man with the paralyzed hand from his disability." What does he want to prove? That "freedom and hope go together: where there's no hope there can be no freedom."

But the real lesson to be drawn from today's liturgy is that Jesus "isn't a healer, he's a man who re-creates lives. And that," stressed the bishop of Rome, "gives us hope, because Jesus came to work that very miracle, to re-create everything." Hence in a most beautiful prayer the church says: "You, Lord, who were so great, so wonderful in creation but even more wonderful in redemption." So, the pope added, "the great miracle is Jesus' great reform. And that gives us hope: Jesus re-creates everything." And "when we join with Jesus in his passion," concluded the pope, "we re-create the world with him, we make it new."

CHRISTIANS WITHOUT FEAR, SHAME, OR TRIUMPHALISM

Tuesday, September 10, 2013
COL 2:6-15; LK 6:12-19

"There are so many Christians without resurrection," in the world today. During the Mass celebrated this morning, Tuesday, September 10, at St. Martha's, the pope invited them to rediscover the way to go towards the risen Jesus, letting themselves "be touched by him, by his strength," because Christ "isn't a spiritual idea"; he is alive. And by his resurrection he has "conquered the world."

Commenting on the readings from the day's liturgy, the pope recalled passages from the letter to the Colossians in which St. Paul speaks of the figure of Jesus, described in them as "the fullness, the center, the hope, because he is the bridegroom." In today's passage (2:6-15) the apostle adds another element, defining Christ as "the conqueror," the one who has "conquered death, sin, the devil." Paul's message contains an invitation to walk in the risen Lord, to be rooted and founded on him, on his victory, firm in faith.

Jesus is "the one who conquers, he's the risen one." But, said the bishop of Rome, often "we don't feel it, we don't hear it well," although Jesus' resurrection is "the very key" to our faith. The pope referred, in particular, to those "Christians without the risen Christ," those who "stay with Jesus up to the tomb, weep, and care so much for him," but who aren't able to go any further. And here he named three sorts: the fearful, the ashamed, and the triumphalist.

The first, he explained, "are those on the morning of the resurrection, those on the road to Emmaus, who leave the city because they are afraid"; they are "the apostles who shut themselves up in the upper room for fear of the Jews"; they are even "those good women who weep," like Mary Magdalene in tears because "they have taken away my Lord." For "the fearful are like that: they're afraid to think of the resurrection." And even the apostles, when Jesus appeared to them in the upper room, "were frightened, fearing that they'd seen a ghost."

The second category is that of the "ashamed. Confessing that Christ is risen makes them feel rather embarrassed in this world that's so advanced in the sciences." According to Pope Francis, they are the ones Paul is thinking about when he warns, "Take care no one deceives you with philosophy or empty deceits inspired by human tradition, according to the ways of the world and not according to Christ." In practice these are the Christians who distort the reality of the resurrection: for them "it's a spiritual resurrection, which does the whole world good, a blessing"; but basically, "they're ashamed to say that Christ is risen in the flesh, with his wounds."

Then the third group are those Christians who at heart "don't believe in the risen Christ and want to make for themselves a nobler resurrection than that" of Jesus. The pope called them "triumphalist," because "they have an inferiority complex" and adopt "triumphalist attitudes in their lives, in their speeches, in their pastoral work and liturgy."

For Pope Francis we need to recover the awareness that Jesus is risen. And to do so, Christians are called upon to gaze "without fear, and without triumphalism," at "his beauty," to put their fingers into his wounds and their hand into the side of "Christ who is all in all, the fullness; Christ who is the center, Christ who is the hope," because he is the bridegroom and the conqueror. And, added the pope, he is "a conqueror who re-creates the whole of creation."

Referring to the passage from Luke's gospel (6:12-19), the Holy Father recalled the image of Jesus among the crowd of men and women who had come "to hear him and be cured of their diseases. And also those who were tormented by unclean spirits came to be cured." So "the whole crowd tried to touch him, because a healing force went out from him." In this Pope Francis sees the assertion of Christ's final victory, which "heals the whole universe," and of "his resurrection." That is why, he concluded, we need to recover the beauty of meeting the risen Christ, and letting ourselves be touched by him, by his healing force.

Contemplating Jesus, Gentle and Suffering

Thursday, September 12, 2013
Col 3:12-17; Lk 6:27-38

It isn't easy for Christians to live a life inspired by Jesus' principles and virtues. "It isn't easy," said Pope Francis during the Mass celebrated this Thursday morning, September 12, in St. Martha's chapel, "but it's possible." All we need to do is "contemplate the suffering Jesus and suffering humanity" and "live a life hidden with Jesus in God."

The Holy Father's reflection took its cue from the liturgical feast of the name of Mary. "Today," he said, "we celebrate Mary's name day. The holy name of Mary. At one time this feast was called the sweet name of Mary, and in our prayer today we asked for the grace to experience Mary's strength and sweetness. Then the title of the feast day was changed but that sweetness of her name has remained in our prayer. Today we need Mary's sweetness in order to understand the things that Jesus asks of us. It's a difficult list to live by: love your enemies, do good, lend without hope of return, if anyone strikes you on the cheek offer your other cheek, if anyone takes your cloak give him your tunic too. These are difficult demands. But in her way all this was done by Mary: she had the grace of gentleness, the grace of mildness."

"The apostle Paul," he continued, "insists on the same thing: 'Brothers, as God's chosen ones, holy and beloved, clothe yourselves with compassion, kindness, humility, meekness and patience. Bear with one another and, if anyone has a complaint against another, forgive each other, just as the Lord has forgiven you' (Colossians 3:12-17)." Certainly, the pope said, a lot is asked of us and so the first spontaneous question that arises is: "But how can I do this? How can I prepare myself to do this? What must I study in order to do this?" For the pope the answer is clear: "We can't do it by our own efforts. Only grace can do it in us. Our own efforts will help; they are necessary but not enough."

"During these days the apostle Paul has often spoken to us of Jesus," continued the pope. "Jesus as the Christian's fullness, Jesus as the Christian's center. Jesus as the Christian's hope, because he is the church's bridegroom and gives us hope to carry on; Jesus as the conqueror of sin and death. Jesus conquers and he went up to heaven with his victory. Here the apostle teaches us something: "He tells us, 'Brothers, if you are risen with Christ, seek the things from above where Christ is triumphant; and sits there at God's right hand. Turn your thoughts to the things above, not things of this earth below... For you have died and your lives are hidden with Christ in God.'"

And this is "the way to do what the Lord asks of us: hide our lives with Christ in God," repeated the pope. And that should be renewed in all our daily attitudes, because only if we have hearts and minds set on the Lord, "who is triumphant over sin and death," can we do what he asks of us.

Gentleness, humility, kindness, tenderness, mildness, and generosity are all virtues which help us to follow the road Christ points to. To receive them is "a grace. A grace which comes from contemplating Jesus." It was not accidental, he reminded us, that our spiritual fathers and mothers taught us how important it is to look at the Lord's passion.

"Only by contemplating Christ's suffering humanity," repeated the pope, "can we become gentle, humble, and tender like him. There's no other way." Of course, we must make the effort to "seek Jesus; to think about his passion, how much he suffered, to think of his submissive silence." This, he repeated, will be our effort. Then "all the rest comes from him and he will supply anything that's missing. But you must do this: hide your life with Christ in God."

So to be good Christians it's necessary always to contemplate Jesus' humanity and all suffering humanity. "To bear witness? Contemplate Jesus. To forgive? Contemplate Jesus' suffering. Not to hate our neighbor? Contemplate Jesus' suffering. Not to gossip against our neighbor? Contemplate Jesus' suffering. There's no other way," repeated the pope, reminding us that these virtues also belong to the Father, "who is kind, gentle, and generous, who always forgives," and also to Mary, our mother. It isn't easy but it's possible. "Let us entrust ourselves to Mary. And when we greet her today on her name day," he concluded, "let us ask her to give us the grace to feel her sweetness."

From Malicious Gossip to Loving Our Neighbor

Friday, September 13, 2013
1 Tim 1:1-2, 12-14; Lk 6:39-42

Gossip kills like a weapon. Worse than a weapon. Pope Francis spoke about this subject again this morning, Friday, September 13, during the Mass celebrated in St. Martha's chapel. Commenting on the readings for the day, taken from the letter to Timothy (1:1-2, 12-14) and from Luke's gospel (6:39-42), the pope pointed out how in the past few days the Lord had spoken about attitudes of gentleness, humility, and generosity, but "today he speaks to us about the opposite," that is, about "an odious attitude towards our neighbors," which we have when we become their "judges."

Pope Francis recalled the gospel episode in which Jesus rebukes someone who tries to take the speck out of another person's eye without seeing the plank in his own. That way of behaving, feeling we're perfect and therefore fit to judge the shortcomings of others, is contrary to the gentleness and humility the Lord tells us about, "to that light which is so beautiful, the light of forgiveness." Jesus, the Holy Father said, "used a strong word: hypocrite." And he stressed: "Those who live by judging their neighbors, speaking ill of them, are hypocrites. Because they lack the strength, the courage to look at their own defects. The Lord doesn't say a lot about this. Then, a bit further on, he says: anyone who has hatred in his heart for his brother is a murderer. He says that. And the apostle John also says very clearly in his first letter: anyone who hates his brother walks in darkness. Anyone who judges his brother is a murderer." Then, the pope added, "Whenever we judge our brothers and sisters in our hearts, or worse when we speak about them to others, we're murderous Christians." And "it's not me saying this but the Lord," for "there's no way of toning this down: if you speak ill of your brother or sister, you kill them. And whenever we do this we become like Cain, the first murderer."

Remember how often we hear of wars in the world today that create victims, especially children, and force many to flee in search of refuge. Pope Francis asked how it is possible to think we have "the right to kill" by speaking ill of others, to unleash "this daily war of gossip." In fact, he said, "malicious gossip always goes in the direction of crime. There's no innocent gossip. And that's the gospel pure and simple." So "at this time when we pray so often for peace perhaps we need an act of conversion." And when we say no to all kinds of weapons, let us also say "no to this other weapon," which is malicious gossip because "it's lethal." Quoting the apostle James, the pope recalled that the tongue "is for praising God." But, he added, "when we use our tongues to speak ill of our brothers and sisters we're using it to kill God," because the image of God is in our brother, in our sister; we're destroying "that image of God."

The Holy Father recalled, there are also those who try to justify all this by saying "they deserve it." The pope gave those people a specific invitation: "Go and pray for him. Go and do penance for her. And then, if necessary, speak to that person who can remedy the problem, but don't tell all the world about it." Paul, added the pope, "was a wicked sinner. And he says of himself: I used to be a sinner, a blasphemer, a violent man. But I received mercy. Perhaps none of us blaspheme. But if any one of us gossips behind another person's back then we are certainly persecuting and being violent." The pope concluded by invoking "for us and for the whole church the grace of conversion from crime, from malicious gossip to humility, gentleness, and generosity of love for our neighbors."

THE TREE OF THE CROSS

Saturday, September 14, 2013
PHIL 2:6-11; JOHN 3:13-17

The story of humanity and the story of God are interwoven on the cross. It's essentially a love story. It's a great mystery, which we can't understand on our own. How can we "taste that aloe honey, the bitter sweetness of Jesus' sacrifice?" Pope Francis told us how this morning, Saturday, September 14, on the feast of the Exaltation of the Holy Cross, during the Mass celebrated in St. Martha's chapel.

Commenting on the readings for the day, taken from the letter to the Philippians (2:6-11) and John's gospel (3:13-17), the pope said it was possible to understand the mystery of the cross "a little bit" when we are "on our knees, in prayer" but also "in tears." For tears "bring us closer to this mystery." Actually, "unless we weep," and above all unless "we weep from the heart, we will never understand this mystery." These are "the tears of the penitent, the tears of the brother or sister, on their knees, weeping, who sees so much human misery and also sees it in Jesus." And above all, said the pope, "never alone!" To enter into this mystery which "isn't a labyrinth but rather like one," we always "need our mother, our mother's hand." Mary, he added, "makes us feel how great and how humble the mystery is, how it's sweet as honey and bitter as aloes."

The fathers of the church, recalled the pope, "always compared the tree of paradise with the tree of the cross." The first tree "did so much harm," whereas the tree of the cross "brings us salvation, health, forgiveness of that wrong." That is "the course of human history," a road that enables us "to find Jesus Christ the redeemer, who gives his life for love." Love that is shown in the economy of salvation, as the Holy Father recalled, according to the words of John the evangelist. In fact, said the pope, God "did not send his Son into the world to condemn the world, but so that the world might be saved through him." And how did he save us? "By that tree of the cross." The other tree was the beginning of "self-sufficiency, pride, and the arrogance of wanting to know everything according to our own way of thinking, according to our own criteria, and the presumption of being and becoming the world's only judges." That, he said, "is the story of humanity." But on the tree of the cross it's God's story, who "wanted to adopt our story and walk with us." And in our first reading of the day Paul "sums up in a few words God's whole story: Jesus Christ, although he was in the form of God, did not regard equality with God as something to be exploited." But "he emptied himself, taking the form of a slave, being born in human likeness." Indeed Christ "humbled himself, becoming obedient to the point of death, death on a cross." That is "the course of God's story." And, asked the bishop of Rome, why does he do it? The answer can be found in Jesus' words to Nicodemus: "God so loved the world that he gave his only begotten Son, so that anyone who believes in him should not perish but have everlasting life." God, he concluded, "does this for love. There's no other explanation."

Pray for Politicians to Govern Us Well

Monday, September 16, 2013
1 Tim 2:1-8; Lk 7:1-10

A good Christian plays an active part in political life and prays that politicians may love their people and serve them with humility. That was the subject of Pope Francis' reflection this morning, Monday, September 16, during the Mass celebrated in St. Martha's chapel.

Commenting on the gospel passage from Luke (7:1-10), which tells the story of the healing by Jesus of the centurion's slave at Capernaum, the pope stressed "two attitudes in a ruler." First of all, he must "love his people. The Jewish elders say to Jesus about the centurion: he deserves what he asks for because he loves our people. A ruler who doesn't love can't rule. At most he can establish some order but he can't rule." And to explain the meaning of the love a ruler should have for his people, the Holy Father recalled the example of David, who disobeyed the census rules laid down in the Mosaic law, to stress that each person's life belongs to the Lord (cf. Exodus 3:11-12). But once he'd understood his sin, David did everything he could to avoid punishment for his people. And that was because, even though he was a sinner, he loved his people.

For Pope Francis a ruler must also be humble like the centurion in the gospel, who could have boasted of his power if he'd asked Jesus to go to his house, but "he was a humble man and said to the Lord: don't trouble yourself, I'm not worthy that you should come under my roof. And he humbly asked: only say the word and my slave will be healed. These are the two virtues of a ruler, as God's word tells us: love for the people and humility."

So "any man or woman who assumes the responsibility of government should ask themselves these two things: Do I love my people to serve them better? Am I humble enough to listen to the opinions of others in order to choose the right way?" For "if they don't ask themselves these questions," stressed the pope, "their government won't be good."

But the governed also need to make the right choices. So what must be done? After noting that we "as a people have so many rulers," the pope recalled a sentence of St. Paul's, taken from the first letter to Timothy (2:1-8): "First of all, then, I urge that supplications, prayers, intercessions and thanksgivings should be made for everyone, for kings and all who are in high positions, so that we may lead a quiet and peaceable life in all godliness and dignity."

That means, said Pope Francis, that "none of us can say: but it's nothing to do with me, they are the ones in government. No, that's not right. I'm responsible for their government and I must do my best to see that they rule well, by participating in politics in the way I can. Politics, according to the church's social teaching, is one of the highest forms of charity, because it's serving the common good. I can't wash my hands of it: each of us must do something. But we're in the habit of thinking that we can just gossip about our rulers, speak ill of them and about things that are going badly."

The Holy Father noted that the television and newspapers mainly "bash" politicians. It's hard to find news that "such and such a politician did well here or that politician has this virtue. He made a mistake about some things but this time he's done well." On the contrary, politicians "are always bad-mouthed, spoken against, always against. Perhaps the politician is a sinner as David was. But I have to take part, with my opinion, my word, also with my corrections: I don't agree with this or that. We should take part in the common good. Sometimes we hear that a good Catholic isn't interested in politics. But that's not true. Good Catholics get involved in politics by offering the best of themselves so that the ruler can rule."

So what is "the best thing we can offer" our rulers? "It's prayer," replied the pope, explaining: "It's what Paul says: pray for the king and for all those who have power." But "it will be said: so and so is a bad person; they should go to hell. No. Pray for him, pray for her, that they may govern well, love their people, be humble. A Christian who doesn't pray for rulers isn't a good Christian. We need to pray. And this, said the pope, isn't me saying so. St. Paul says so. May rulers be humble and love their people. That's the condition. That we, the governed, give of our best. Above all by prayer."

"Let us pray for rulers," concluded Pope Francis, "to govern well. May they forward our country, our nation and also the world. And may we have peace and the common good. May this word of God help us to participate better in our people's common life: for those who govern let it be a service of humility and love; and let those who are governed participate and above all pray."

Like a Mother Defending Her Children

Tuesday, September 17, 2013
1 Tim 3:1-13; Lk 7:11-17

Like a mother who loves us, defends us, gives us the strength to carry on in the fight against evil. That was the image of the church described by Pope Francis today, Tuesday, September 17, during the Mass celebrated early this morning at St. Martha's.

Commenting on the gospel passage from Luke that tells the story of the raising of the widow's son at Nain (7:11-17), the pope described Jesus who, when he saw the woman standing by the corpse of her only son, "was filled with compassion." The pope described Christ's feeling as "the capacity to suffer with us, to be close to us in our sufferings and make them his own." Besides, he knew very well "what it meant to be a widow at that time," when mothers left to bring up their children alone had to rely on the charity of others. That commandments at that time stressed so strongly: "Help orphans and widows, because at that time they were the most lonely and abandoned."

The bishop of Rome then turned his thoughts to other widows in the Bible. The Lord has a special "care for them, a special love," so that they end up being "an image of the church because," he explained, "the church is also a sort of widow: her husband has gone away and she goes through history hoping to find him again, to be reunited with him. Then once and for all she will be his wife." But, he said, "in the meantime the church is alone," and the Lord is not visible to her, so "she's a sort of widow."

The first consequence of this widowhood is that the church should become "brave" like a mother "who defends her children," like the widow in the gospel "who went to an unjust judge to defend her children and in the end she won." For, stressed the pope, "our mother the church has the courage of a woman who knows that these children are hers and she must defend them and bring them to meet her husband."

Courage gives her strength, as we see from other widows described in scripture. For example Naomi, David's great-grandmother, "who wasn't afraid to be alone," or the Maccabean widow with seven sons, "who refused to deny God or God's law and were martyred by the tyrant." One thing in particular about this woman struck Pope Francis: the fact that the Bible says "she spoke in dialect, in her mother tongue," just as "our mother the church does," who speaks to us "in that language of true orthodoxy we all understand, the language of the catechism, that strong language, which makes us strong and also gives us the strength to carry on in the fight against evil."

Summing up his own reflections, the pope repeated "the way in which the church is like a widow going through history hoping to meet, to find her husband." And, he said, "our mother the church is like that; when she is faithful she's a church that knows how to cry, to cry for her children and pray." So "when the church doesn't cry, something isn't right." Whereas the church is working properly when she "carries on letting children grow, giving them strength, staying with them to the end, in order to leave them in the hands of her husband, whom she too finally will meet."

And since the pope sees "our mother the church in that weeping widow," we need to ask what the Lord says to that mother to comfort her. The answer is in the words of Jesus reported by Luke: "Don't weep!" Words which seem to say don't weep, because "I am with you, I stand by you, I am waiting for you there at the wedding, the final wedding, the wedding of the Lamb." Stop crying, "this your son who was dead is now alive." And to this third person present in the gospel story the Lord turns and says: "Young man, I say to you: rise!" For the pope these are the same words as the Lord addresses to people in the sacrament of reconciliation, "when we're dead through sin and go and ask him for forgiveness."

Luke's story ends with the description of the dead young man sitting up and beginning to speak. Then Jesus gives him back to his mother. Just as he does with us, noted the pope, "when he forgives us, when he gives us our life back," because "our reconciliation doesn't end with the conversation," with the priest who gives us absolution, but becomes complete "when he restores us to our mother." In fact, the pope concluded, "there's no way forward in life, no forgiveness, no reconciliation outside our mother the church." So we must always "ask the Lord for the grace to feel confident in this mother who defends us, teaches us, and enables us to grow."

THE POWER OF MONEY

Friday, September 20, 2013
1 TIM 6:2-12; LK 8:1-3

We must guard against giving in to the temptation to idolize money. That would weaken our faith and risk becoming addicted to the deception of senseless and harmful desires that lead people to wrack and ruin. Pope Francis warned against this danger during his homily in the Mass celebrated this morning, Friday, September 20, in St. Martha's chapel.

"Jesus," said the Holy Father commenting on the day's readings, "told us clearly that we can't serve two masters: we can't serve God and money. It won't work. Something about loving money distances us from God." And quoting Paul's first letter to Timothy (6:2-12), the pope said: "But those who want to be rich fall into temptation and are trapped by many senseless and harmful desires that plunge people into ruin and destruction."

In fact, he continued, "greed is the root of all evils. Gripped by this desire, some people have strayed from the faith and caused themselves a lot of grief. The power of money is so strong that it turns you away from true faith. It cuts you off from faith, weakens it and you lose it." And staying with the letter to Timothy, the pope noted that the apostle also says: "Whoever teaches otherwise and does not agree with the sound words of our Lord Jesus

Christ and the teaching that is in accordance with godliness, is conceited, understanding nothing, and has a morbid craving for controversy and for disputes about words."

But St. Paul goes even further, noted the pope, and he writes: "From these come envy, dissension, slander, base suspicions, and wrangling among those who are depraved in mind and bereft of the truth, imagining that godliness is a means of gain."

The bishop of Rome then referred to all those who say they are Catholics because they go to Mass, those who regard their being Catholics as a status and who "beneath it all pursue their own business." Here, the pope recalled, Paul uses a particular term which "we so often find in the newspapers: corrupt, corrupt minds! Money corrupts. There's no way out of this. If you opt for the way of money, you will end up becoming corrupt. Money can lure you so that you slowly slide into perdition. That's why Jesus is so firm: you can't serve God and money. It can't be done. It's either one or the other. And that's not communism, it's the gospel pure and simple. These are the words of Jesus."

So "what happens with money?" asked the pope. "Money," he replied, "gives you a certain sense of well-being: you are well off, you feel a bit important and then comes vanity. We have read it in the Psalm 49: you get this vanity. This vanity that is worthless but makes you feel like an important person." Vanity, pride, wealth: that's what the people mentioned in the psalm boast of: those who "trust in their wealth and boast of the abundance of their riches." But what is the truth? The truth, explained the pope, is that "no ransom avails for one's life; there's no price one can give to God for it. For the ransom of life is costly, and can never suffice that one should live on forever and never see the grave," even though the temptation may be strong to pursue "wealth to feel self-sufficient, vanity to feel important, and finally, pride and arrogance."

The pope then spoke of the sin linked to lust for money, with all that it entails. In the first of the Ten Commandments it's the sin of "idolatry," he said. "Money," he explained, "becomes an idol and you worship it. And that's why Jesus tells us: you can't serve the idol money and the living God. It's either the one or the other." The early fathers of the church "used a strong expression: money is the devil's dung. It is so because it makes us idolatrous and sickens our minds with pride and a weakness for idle questions and distances us from the faith. It corrupts." But the apostle Paul tells us to go for justice, godliness, faith, love, endurance, gentleness. Against vanity, against pride "serve gentleness." So "that's God's way, not the way of idolatrous power that money can give you. It's Jesus Christ's way of humility, who was rich and became poor to enrich us by his poverty. That's the way to serve God. And may the Lord help us all not to fall into the trap of idolizing money."

Like Blowing on Embers

Saturday, September 21, 2013
Eph 4:1-7, 11-13; Mt 9:9-13

The way Jesus looks at you makes you grow, go forward; it encourages you because it makes you feel that he loves you; it gives you the courage necessary to follow him. Pope Francis focused on the way Jesus looks at us in his meditation during the Mass at St. Martha's this morning, Saturday, September 21. This is an important date in Jorge Mario Bergoglio's life, because sixty years ago on St. Matthew's feast day—it was September 21, 1953—he chose the life he would lead. Perhaps that was another reason why, in commenting on the story of the evangelist's conversion (Matthew 9:9-13), the pope stressed the power of the way

Jesus looked at people, a look that was able to change forever the lives of those he looked at.

That is what happened to the tax collector who became a disciple. "It's a bit difficult for me to understand how Matthew was able to hear Jesus' voice," saying amidst all those people "follow me." The bishop of Rome wasn't actually sure that the man who was called had heard the voice of Jesus, but he was sure that he'd "felt in his heart the look that Jesus gave him. And it was also a face" that "changed his life. We say: it converted him." There is also another action described in the scene: "As soon as he felt that look in his heart, he got up and followed Jesus." For, the pope noted, "Jesus looking at us always makes us get up, it pulls us up," it rouses us; but "it leaves us there" where we were before we met him. Neither does it take anything from us. "It never lowers you, it never humiliates you, it invites you to get up," and by making you feel his love, it gives you the necessary courage to be able to follow him.

So this was the pope's question: "What was there about the way Jesus looked at people?" His answer was, "it wasn't a magic look," since Christ "wasn't a specialist in hypnosis," but quite different. We need only think of how "he looked at the sick and healed them" or "he looked at the crowd and felt sorry for them, because he felt they were like sheep without a shepherd." And above all, according to the Holy Father in answer to his question, we need to think not only "about the way Jesus looked at people" but also about "how people felt" when he looked at them. Because, he explained, "Jesus looked at everybody," and "and everyone felt they were being looked at by him," as if he were calling each of them by name.

So Christ's look "changes lives." Everybody's life in every situation. Also in moments of difficulty and distress, Pope Francis added. As when he asked his disciples: do you also want to go away? He was looking them "in the eye and they were encouraged to say no, we're coming with you." Or as when Peter had denied him, Jesus looked at him again, "which changed his heart and made him weep bitterly: Jesus' look changed everything." And finally "Jesus' last look," when from high on the cross "he looked at his mother, and the beloved disciple." By that look "he told us that his mother was our mother, and the church is our mother." So that is why "it does us good to think, to pray about that look of Jesus and let him look at us."

Pope Francis then returned to the gospel scene, which continues with Jesus sitting at table with publicans and sinners. "The word spread and all and sundry, the whole society, but not 'polite' society, felt invited to that meal," commented Pope Francis, because "Jesus had looked at them, and that look had been like someone blowing on embers; they had felt there was fire inside them." And they had also felt that "Jesus made them get up"; it roused them, "it gave them back their dignity," because "Jesus' look always makes us worthy, gives us dignity."

Then the pope pointed out a final characteristic in Jesus' look: generosity. He is a teacher who lunches with the city lowlife, but who also knows how "under that dirt lie the embers of a desire for God." They want someone "to help them blaze." And that's just what "Jesus' look does": then as it does today. "I believe that all of us in our lives," said Pope Francis, "have felt that look, not just once but many times. Perhaps in the person of a priest, who taught us or forgave our sins, perhaps from a friend who helped us." And finally, "all of us will stand before that look, that wonderful look." So "let us carry on in life, in the certainty that he is looking at us and he is waiting for us to look at us finally. And that final look at our life by Jesus will be forever; it will be conclusive." We can ask for help in prayer from all "the saints who were looked at by Jesus," so that "we may prepare to let ourselves be looked at in our lives and also prepare ourselves for Jesus to look at us finally."

A Traveling Companion

Tuesday, September 24, 2013
Ez 6:7-8, 14-20; Lk 8:19-21

A sacrament isn't a "magic rite" but the means God has chosen with which to walk beside us as a traveling companion in life, to make history together with us, waiting for us if necessary. And faced with that divine humility, we must have the courage to let him write history, which thereby becomes "reliable." The certainty of God's continual presence in human events was the focus of the homily given by Pope Francis on this morning of Tuesday, September 24, during the Mass celebrated in St. Martha's chapel.

The pope began by repeating the invocation in Psalm 122 (121), proclaimed during the liturgy: "We shall go joyfully to the house of the Lord." And "we have done this," he explained, "because the first reading reminds us of a moment of joy for the people of God. Such a beautiful moment!" It was the moment when "a pagan king helped the people of God to return to their land to rebuild the temple." The story is in a passage in the book of Ezra (6:7-8, 14-20).

"In the story of the people of God," continued Pope Francis, "there are beautiful moments like this one, which give so much joy, and also terrible moments of pain, martyrdom, and sin. God never abandons his people, because on that day of sin, the first sin, the Lord took a decision, he made a choice: to make history with his people."

"God, who has no history because he is eternal," added the pope, "wanted to make history, to walk beside his people. But there's more: he wanted to become one of us, walk with us as one of us, in Jesus. And this speaks to us, this tells us about God's humility." He is "so great" and powerful precisely because, in his humility, he "wanted to walk with his people. And when his people distanced themselves from him by sin, by idolatry, so many things we find in the Bible, God was there."

An attitude of humility that we also recognize in Jesus, explained the pope: "walking with the people of God, walking with sinners, also walking with the proud: what a lot the Lord did to help the proud hearts of the Pharisees. He wanted to walk with us. Humility. God always waits. God is beside us. God walks with us, he is humble. He always waits for us. Jesus always waits for us. That's God's humility."

So, added the pope, "the church sings with joy of this humility of God who walks with us. As we sang in the psalm: 'We shall go joyfully to the house of the Lord.' We shall go joyfully, he accompanies us, he is with us."

"The Lord Jesus," he stressed, "also accompanies us in our personal lives through the sacraments. The sacrament isn't a magic rite, it's a meeting with Jesus Christ"; in it "we meet the Lord. And he is beside us and walks with us as a traveling companion." And "the Holy Spirit also accompanies us and teaches us everything we don't know in our hearts. He reminds us of everything Jesus taught us and makes us feel the beauty of the right road. And so God: Father, Son, and Holy Spirit are our traveling companions. They enter into history with us."

"The church," Pope Francis said again, "celebrates this with such joy in the Eucharist." And he recalled "that beautiful eucharistic prayer which we will pray today, when we sing of the great love of God who wanted to be humble, who wanted to be the traveling companion of all of us, who also wanted to enter into history with us." And, he concluded, "if he's entered our story, let us also enter a little into his story, or at least let us ask him for the grace to let him write the story himself. Let him write our story for us. That is reliable."

PRAYER FOR PEACE IN THE MIDDLE EAST

Wednesday, September 25, 2013
Ez 9:5-9; Lk 9:1-6

Shame before God, prayer to implore God's mercy and full trust in the Lord. These were the main points of Pope Francis' reflection this morning, Wednesday, September 25, during the Mass celebrated in St. Martha's chapel. The Mass was concelebrated with Cardinals Leonardo Sandri, prefect of the Congregation for the Eastern Churches, and Béchara Boutros Raï, Maronite patriarch of Antioch, together with a group of Maronite bishops from Lebanon, Syria, the Holy Land, and various other countries from every continent.

In commenting on the readings in the liturgy (Ezra 9:5-9; Luke 9:1-6), the Holy Father said that the passage from the book of Ezra, in particular, made him think about the Maronite bishops, and as usual, he summed up his thinking with three points. First, Ezra's attitude of shame and confusion before God, so that he couldn't raise his eyes toward him. Shame and confusion of all of us for the sins we have committed, which have brought us into slavery because we have served idols who are not God.

Second, there was prayer. Following Ezra's example, who knelt and lifted his hands up to God imploring him for mercy, we should also do the same for our countless sins. And, said the pope, our prayer should also be for peace in Lebanon, Syria, and the whole of the Middle East. Prayer, he said, is always the way we must face difficult times, the hardest trials, and the darkness that sometimes envelops us in unpredictable situations. To find a way out of all that, stressed the pope, we must pray without ceasing.

Last, absolute trust in God who never abandons us. That was the third point made by the Holy Father. Let us be certain, he said, that the Lord is with us, and so we should persevere on our way, thanks to the hope that gives us strength. Pastors can reassure the faithful: the Lord will never abandon us.

After the communion, Cardinal Béchara Raï thanked the Holy Father and gave him a very warm greeting from the bishops present, from all the Maronites and Lebanon as a whole. He confirmed their faithfulness to Peter and his successor "who sustains us on our way, which is often thorny." In particular, he thanked the pope for the strong impulse he has given to the quest for peace: "His prayer and exhortation for peace in Syria and the Middle East has sown hope and comfort."

Knowing Jesus

Thursday, September 26, 2013
Hag 1:1-8; Lk 9:7-9

Really knowing Jesus means speaking with him, conversing with him while we follow him along his way. Knowing Jesus was the focus of Pope Francis' homily during the Mass celebrated this morning, Thursday, September 26, in St. Martha's chapel.

The pope took his cue from the gospel passage in Luke (9:7-9), in which Herod asks who is Jesus, about whom he has heard so much. The person of Jesus, recalled the pope, often aroused questions such as "Who is he? Where does he come from? Think of Nazareth, for example, of the synagogue at Nazareth when Jesus spoke in it for the first time. But where did he learn those things? We know him well: he's the carpenter's son. Think of Peter and the apostles after that storm, that wind which Jesus calmed. But who is he whom heaven and earth, wind, rain and storm obey? Who is he?"

Questions, explained the pope, that can be asked out of curiosity or to know how to behave toward him. But the fact remains that whoever meets Jesus asks these questions. So "some people," continued the pope returning to the gospel story, "began to be afraid of this man, because he might bring them into political conflict with the Romans." And so they decided not to have anything more to do with "this man who causes so many problems."

And, asked the pope, why does Jesus create problems? "You can't meet Jesus," he replied, "without having problems." Paradoxically, he added, "if you want to have a problem, go the way that leads you to meet Jesus." Then all kinds of problems will arise. In any case, you can't meet Jesus sitting "in first class" or "in peace and quiet," even less "in a library." Jesus can be met only on the road of daily life.

We can also know him, said the Holy Father, "in the catechism. It's true! The catechism teaches us so many things about Jesus and we must study it, we must learn it. Thus we learn that God's Son came to save us and we understand God's love from the beauty of the story of salvation." However, the fact remains that knowing Jesus through the catechism "isn't enough": knowing him with our minds is a step forward, "but we need to know Jesus by conversing with him. By talking with him, in prayer, on our knees. If you don't pray, if you don't speak with Jesus," he said, "you don't know him."

Lastly, there is a third way of knowing Jesus: "It's the sequel, going with him, walking with him, going his way." And when we walk with him, we know "Jesus in the language of action. If you know Jesus in these three languages—mind, heart, and action—then you can say that you know Jesus." That kind of knowledge requires personal involvement. "You can't know Jesus," repeated the pope, "without becoming involved with him, without committing your life to him." So to know him truly it's necessary to read "what the church tells you about him, speak with him in prayer, and walk his way with him." That is the way and "everyone," he concluded, "must make their own choice."

THE WAY OF JESUS

Friday, September 27, 2013
HAG 2:1-9; LK 9:18-22

The choice is between being "comfort Christians" or "Christians who follow Jesus." Comfort Christians are those who think they have everything if they have the church, the sacraments, the saints... The others are Christians who follow Jesus to the end, to the humiliation of the cross and bear this humiliation serenely. That was the focus of Pope Francis' reflection this morning, Friday, September 27, in his homily during the Mass celebrated in St. Martha's chapel.

The Holy Father picked up on what he'd said yesterday about the different ways of knowing Jesus: "with the mind, with the catechism, with prayer and what follows." And he recalled the question with which this quest to know Jesus began: "But who is he?" However, today "it's Jesus himself who asks the question," as we hear in today's gospel passage from Luke (9:18-22). Jesus' question, the pope noted, began as a general one—"who do people say that I am?"—and becomes a question addressed to specific people, in this case to the apostles: "But who do you say that I am?" And this question, he continued, "is also addressed to us at this moment, when the Lord is among us, at this celebration, in his word, in the eucharist on the altar, in his sacrifice. Today he asks each one of us: who am I for you? The owner of this company? A good prophet? A good teacher? Someone who does your heart good? Someone who walks with you in life, who helps you go forward, to be somewhat good? Yes, all that is true, but that's not the end of it," because "it was the Holy Spirit who touched Peter's heart and made him say who Jesus was: You are the Christ, the Son of the living God." Any of us, the pope continued, "who looks at the tabernacle and says to the Lord in prayer: you are the Christ, the Son of the living God," must know two things. The first is: "you can't say this of your own accord; it has to be the Holy Spirit saying it in you." The second thing is that you have to be prepared, "because he will answer you."

The Holy Father then described the different attitudes a Christian can adopt: to follow him up to a certain point, or to follow him to the end. The risk we run, he warned, was to give way to "the temptation of spiritual comfort," to think we have everything: the church, Jesus Christ, the sacraments, the Madonna and so we don't need to seek anything else. If we think like that, "we're good people, because we need to believe that at the very least; if we think otherwise it's a 'sin.'" But that "isn't enough. Spiritual comfort," the pope explained, "is all right up to a point." But what's lacking in order to be a true Christian is "the anointing of the cross, the anointing of humiliation. He humiliated himself to the point of death, death on a cross. That's the touchstone, the test of how really Christian we are. Am I a comfort Christian or am I a Christian who accompanies the Lord right to the cross? To know whether we belong to those who accompany Jesus right to the cross, the test is "the ability to bear humiliations. Christians who don't go with this program of the Lord are halfway Christians: lukewarm. They are good people; they do good things." But they won't bear the humiliations. They keep asking, "Why does he get the break and not me? Humiliation isn't for me. And why does that happen to him and not to me? And why do they make that person a monsignor and not me?"

"Let's remember James and John," the pope continued, "when

they asked the Lord for honors. You don't know, you don't understand anything, the Lord told them. The choice is clear: the Son of Man has to suffer many things, be rejected by the elders, by the chief priests and the scribes, be killed and rise again on the third day."

"But what about us? We want the last bit to happen. We all want to rise again on the third day. That's right, that's good, we should want that." But not all of us, said the pope, are ready to go the way to get there, the way of Jesus; they think it's a scandal if someone does something to them which they regard as a wrong, and they complain about it. So the sign by which to tell "if a Christian is a real Christian" is "their capacity to bear humiliations with joy and patience." That is "something we don't like," stressed Pope Francis. And yet "there are so many Christians who look at the Lord and ask for humiliations so that they may become more like him."

Fear of the Cross

Saturday, September 28, 2013
Zech 2:5-9, 14-15a; Lk 9:43b-45

The cross is frightening. But following Jesus inevitably means accepting the cross that faces every Christian. And we should ask Mary—she knows how to stand beside the cross because she stood there—how not to run away from it, even if we are afraid. That was Pope Francis' reflection this morning, Saturday, September 28, during the Mass celebrated in St. Martha's chapel.

Commenting on the passage from Luke in the liturgy of the day (9:43-45), the Holy Father recalled that at the time the evangelist was speaking about how "Jesus was busy with so many ac-

tivities and everyone admired all the things he did. He was the
'leader of the moment.' All Judea, Galilee, and Samaria were talking about him. And just at the point when his disciples were enjoying this, Jesus said to them: Be fully aware of this: the Son of
Man will be delivered into the hands of men."

At the moment of triumph, noted the pope, Jesus announces
his passion. However, the disciples were so taken up with the
festive atmosphere "that they didn't understand his words; they
were so mysterious to them that they didn't grasp their meaning."
And, he continued, "they didn't ask for explanations. The gospel
says they were afraid to ask him about it." So, better not to talk
about it. Better "not to understand the truth." They were afraid
of the cross.

In fact, even Jesus himself was afraid but, explained the pope,
"he didn't deceive himself. He knew. And he was so afraid that on
that Thursday evening he sweat blood." He asked God: "Father,
take away this cup from me," but then he added, "your will be
done. And that's the difference. The cross frightens us."

This is also what happens when we commit ourselves to wit-
nessing to the gospel and to following Jesus. "We are all happy,"
noted the pope, but we don't ask ourselves about it; we don't
speak about the cross. And yet, he continued, as there is "a rule
that the disciple isn't greater than the master"—a rule to be respected—there is also the rule that "there's no redemption without shedding of blood." And "there's no fruitful apostolic work
without the cross." Each of us, he explained, "perhaps may wonder: and what about me? What will my cross be like? We don't
know, but it will come and we must ask for the grace not to run
away from the cross when it comes. Of course it frightens us, but
that's where following Jesus leads. Jesus' words to Peter come to
mind, when he gave him his mission: 'Do you love me? Feed...
Do you love me? Feed... Do you love me? Feed...'" (cf. John
21:15-17). And "his final words were the same: they will take

you where you don't want to go. He was foretelling the cross."

And so, the Holy Father concluded, returning to the gospel passage in the liturgy, "that's why the disciples were afraid to question him. His mother stood very close to Jesus on the cross. Perhaps today, a day on which we pray to her, it would be good to ask her for the grace to banish our fear because fear will come. Let us ask her for the grace not to run away from the cross. She was there and she knows how to stand close to the cross."

THE AIR OF THE CHURCH

Monday, September 30, 2013
ZECH 8:1-8; LK 9:46-50

Peace and joy: "that's the air of the church." Commenting on the readings at the Mass celebrated this morning, Monday, September 30, in St. Martha's chapel, Pope Francis spoke about the atmosphere we breathe when the church is aware of the Lord's constant presence. An atmosphere of peace, where the Lord's joy reigns.

The readings were from the book of Zechariah (8:1-8)—the prophecy that the streets of Jerusalem would be filled again with old folk with their walking sticks showing how long they'd lived, and young folk playing happily to show the joy of the people of God—and from a passage in Luke's gospel (9:46-50), which tells of the dispute between the apostles about who would be greatest among them.

In the two passages the pope saw a sort of discussion, or rather, an exchange of opinions about the organization of the church. But, he recalled, "the Lord likes to surprise us," and so "he shifts the focus of the discussion." He sets a child by his side and says:

Whoever welcomes this child in my name welcomes me. For the least among all of you is the greatest." But the disciples didn't understand.

"In the first reading," said the pope, "we heard God's promise to his people: I will return to Zion, I will dwell in Jerusalem and Jerusalem will be called the faithful city. The Lord will return." But "what are the signs that the Lord has returned? Good organization? A government that runs smoothly, with everything in order?" he asked. For his answer the Holy Father returned to the image of the streets of Jerusalem crowded with old people and children.

So "those whom we leave aside when we think of an organization program," he said, "will be the sign of God's presence: old people and children. Old people because they have wisdom, the wisdom gained during their lifetime, the wisdom of tradition, the wisdom of history, the wisdom of God's law; and children because they are also strength, the future; they will bring the future with their life and energy."

That's where a people's future lies, repeated Pope Francis, "in the old and in children. A country that doesn't take care of its old folk and its children has no future, because it will have no memory and no promise. Old people and children are a country's future."

Unfortunately, he added, "we're accustomed to fobbing children off with a sweet or a toy." Just as we're accustomed to not allowing old people to speak "and taking no notice of their advice." And yet Jesus tells us to pay great attention to children, not to scandalize them; and he also reminded us that "the only commandment that carries a blessing with it is the fourth: to honor our fathers and mothers, our old people."

Naturally, the disciples wanted "the church to carry on without problems. But that," the pope warned, "can become a temptation for the church: the 'functionalist' church, the well-organized church. Everything in order." But it isn't like that, because it would be a church "with no memory and no promise." And of course that "can't work."

"The prophet," continued the Holy Father, "tells us about the church's vitality. But he doesn't say: I will be with you and every week you will have a document to consider; every month we'll have a planning meeting." All that, he added, is necessary, but it isn't the sign of God's presence. The Lord tells us what that sign is: "Old men and old women shall again sit in the streets of Jerusalem, each with a stick in hand because of their great age. And the streets of the city shall be full of boys and girls playing in its streets."

"Playing," concluded the bishop of Rome, "makes us think of joy. It's the Lord's joy. And those old people sitting with a walking stick in their hand make us think of peace. Peace and joy, that's the air of the church."

THE HUMILITY AND POWER OF THE GOSPEL

The Pope Invites Us to Pray for the Work of the Council of Cardinals

Tuesday, October 1, 2013
ZECH 8:20-23; LK 9:51-56

"The Council of Cardinals is beginning its meeting in the Vatican today. They are already here concelebrating in this Mass. Let us ask the Lord that our work today may make us all humbler, gentler, more patient, and more trusting in God. For thus the church can bear witness to people. And when they see the people of God, see the church, they may feel the urge to come with us." These were the concluding words of Pope Francis to his homily at the Mass celebrated with the members of the Council of Cardinals on Tuesday morning, October 1, in St. Martha's chapel. And on the feast day of St. Terese of the Child Jesus, patron of missions, the pope remembered her witness of faith and humility.

Pope Francis began his homily by commenting on the gospel passage from Luke (9:51-56): "Jesus," he said, "rebukes these two apostles," James and John, "because they wanted to bring down fire from heaven on those who didn't welcome them" in a Samaritan village. And "perhaps they were thinking of the fire that fell on Sodom and Gomorrah and destroyed everything." The two apostles, explained the pope, "felt that it was a great insult to shut the door on Jesus; these people must be punished." But "the Lord turned and rebuked them: that isn't our spirit." In fact, added Pope Francis, "the Lord always goes ahead, he shows us the Christian way. And it isn't, in this case, a way of revenge. The Christian spirit isn't like that, says the Lord. It's the spirit that he shows us at the most important moment of his life, in his passion: a spirit of humility, a spirit of gentleness."

"And today, on the feast of St. Therese of the Child Jesus," said the bishop of Rome, "it will do us good to think about this spirit of humility, tenderness, kindness. That gentle spirit of the Lord that he wants all of us to share. Where can we find the power to lead us to this spirit? In love, in charity, in the awareness that we are in the Father's hands. As we read at the beginning of the Mass, the Lord carries us, he carries us on, he keeps us going, he is with us, he leads us."

Pope Francis recalled the strength of St. Therese of the Child Jesus and her relevance today: "This saint was humble, gentle, she trusted in God. The church in its wisdom has made her patron of missions. That isn't easy to understand. But the power of the gospel is there, because the gospel reaches its climax in the humiliation of Jesus. Humility becomes humiliation. And the power of the gospel lies in that humility. A child's humility who allows herself to be led by the Father's love and tenderness."

Then the pope went back to the first reading of the Mass, taken from the book of Zechariah (8:20-23). "In those days ten men from nations of every language shall take hold of a Jew, grasping his garment and saying, 'Let us go with you, for we have heard God is with you.'" And the pope continued: "Benedict XVI told us that the church grows by attraction, by witness. And when people, nations, see this witness of humility, gentleness, mildness, they feel the need" that "the prophet Zechariah speaks of: 'We want to go with you!' People feel that need when they see the witness of charity. It's that public charity without show, that doesn't boast but which is humble, that worships and serves. Charity is simple: worshiping God and serving others. That witness is what makes the church grow." That is why, concluded Pope Francis, St. Therese of the Child Jesus, "who was so humble but so trusting in God, was appointed patron of missions, because her example makes people say: we want to come with you."

The Joy of Christian Memory

Thursday, October 3, 2013
Neh 8:1-4a, 5-6, 7b-12; Lk 10:1-12

Christians who turn the memory of salvation history brought by Jesus into a mere record lose awareness of the value of one of the fundamental principles of the Christian faith: memory that brings joy. And so they experience the Eucharist, which is the memory that makes the church, as a boring social event. This is what Pope Francis said, commenting on the first reading of the Mass celebrated this morning, Thursday, October 3, in St. Martha's chapel.

The reading, taken from the book of Nehemiah (8:1-4, 5-6, 7-12), describes the re-finding of the book of the law, which had been lost, and Ezra reading it before the people of God. "They were so moved," noted the pope, "that they wept. They wept for joy, they wept for love," because the lost book had been found. This means that "the people of God had the memory of the law," explained the pope. But "it was a distant memory."

The reading from the book brings back the people's memory. And thus, while Ezra read and the Levites explained the words of the law, "the people said: amen, amen." They cried "for joy," said the Holy Father, "not from pain. They cried for joy because they experienced the memory afresh, the memory of salvation struck home. And that's important not only at the great historical moments, but also at moments in our lives."

We all have the memory of salvation, the pope declared. But, he asked, "is our memory of it fresh? Or is it a distant, rather vague memory, a bit dusty, like something in a museum?" When the memory isn't fresh, when we no longer feel the memory as a fresh experience, little by little it becomes "a mere record. That's why Moses told the people: go to the temple every year, remember where you came from, how you were saved." Refreshing the memory of our salvation stirs joy in us. "And that," said the bishop of Rome "is the people's joy. It's a principle of Christian life. The Levites calmed down the people who were weeping with emotion and repeated: don't be sad, don't be sad, because the joy you are feeling now is the Lord's joy and it is your strength."

When a memory is fresh, repeated the pope, "it does two things: it warms the heart and it gives joy," whereas "stale memory becomes distant and becomes a mere record; it doesn't warm the heart, it doesn't give us joy, and it doesn't give us strength." Meeting with memory "is a salvation event, a meeting with the love of God, who has made history with us and saved us. It's so lovely to be saved that we must celebrate." For "when God comes, when he comes near," he added, "it's always a celebration."

Nevertheless, so often "we Christians are afraid of celebrating" and life often distances us from our memory; "we merely keep a record of salvation, not the living memory of it. The church, stressed Pope Francis, keeps her own memory, in what we're about to do in this Mass, her memory of the Lord's passion. That same Lord who said to us: do this in memory of me. But sometimes we too distance that memory and make it just a record, a habit. We go to church every week, or someone we know has died and we go to the funeral. And that memory sometimes bores us, because it isn't fresh to us. Sadly, so often the Mass becomes just a social event."

That means we aren't alive to the church's memory, which is the presence of the Lord with us. "Imagine," continued the pope, "that beautiful scene in the book of Nehemiah. Ezra brings the book of Israel's memory and the people get close to their memory and weep. Their hearts are warmed, they are joyful, they feel that the Lord's joy is his strength and they simply celebrate, without fear."

"Let us ask the Lord," the Holy Father concluded, "for the grace always to keep his memory fresh to us—a memory that is fresh and has not grown stale from habit, from so many things, and so distant as to become a mere record."

RUNNING AWAY FROM GOD

Monday, October 7, 2013
JON 1:1–2:1, 11; LK 10:25-37

To hear God's voice in our own lives we need to have a heart open to surprises. Otherwise we risk "running away from God," perhaps giving a good excuse. And so it can happen that we Christians are tempted to run away from God, and those who are "far off" manage to listen to him. That is what Pope Francis said when he celebrated Mass on Monday morning, October 7, at St. Martha's. He suggested a safe road: let our story be written by God.

In his homily the bishop of Rome commented on the first reading, from the story of Jonah (1:1-2:1, 11). Jonah "had his whole life well organized: he served the Lord, perhaps he prayed frequently. He was a prophet, he was a good man, he did good." Since "he didn't want to be disturbed in the way of life he'd chosen, at the very moment when he heard God's word, he began to run away. He ran away from God." So when "the Lord sent him to Nineveh, he took ship for Spain. He fled from the Lord."

After all, explained the pope, Jonah had already written his own story: "I want to be like this and this and this, according to the commandments." He didn't want to be disturbed. That is why he "ran away from God." A flight, the pope warned, that we also see happening today. "We can run away from God," he said, "even when we're Christians, even when we're Catholics," even "a priest, bishop, or pope. We can all run away from God, not listen to his voice, not hear in our hearts what he's asking, what he's inviting us to do."

And if "we can take direct flight," he continued, "there are also other ways of running away from God, which are rather more sophisticated, more polite." He referred to the gospel passage from Luke (10:25-37), which tells the story of "this half-dead man lying in the street. By chance a priest was going along the same road. A worthy priest, wearing a cassock, an excellent man. He saw and he looked. I'll be late for Mass and he passed by on the other side. He didn't hear God's voice there." That, explained the pope, "is a different sort of running away: not like Jonah who just fled. Then a Levite went by, he saw and perhaps he thought: 'But if I pick him up, if I approach him, perhaps he's dead and tomorrow I'll have to go before the judge and be a witness.' And he passed by on the other side. He ran away from God's voice in that man."

On the other hand, it was "odd" that the only one "able to hear God's voice" was a man "who habitually ran away from God, a sinner." In fact, explained the pope, "the one who heard God's voice and approached" the man needing help "was a Samaritan, a sinner," who was far from God. A man, he remarked, "who wasn't accustomed to religious practices or to a moral life." He was theologically in error because Samaritans believed that God should be worshiped elsewhere" and not in Jerusalem.

But it was this person who "understood God was calling him and didn't run away." He became "a neighbor" to the man in trouble, "bandaging his wounds and pouring oil and wine on them. Then he mounted him on his own animal. But what a lot of time he lost! He took him to an inn and took care of him. He lost the whole afternoon!" Meanwhile, noted the bishop of Rome, "the priest arrived in time for Mass and all the faithful were happy. The Levite had a peaceful next day, as he had planned" because he didn't have to go to the judge.

"And why," asked the pope, "did Jonah run away from God? Why did the Levite run away from God? Because," he replied, "their hearts were closed. When your heart is closed, you can't hear God's voice. Whereas the Samaritan, who was traveling, saw that wounded man and "felt sorry for him. He had an open heart, he was human." And his humanity brought him close to the wounded man.

"Jonah," he explained, "had a plan for his life: he wanted to write his story well, in accordance with God. But he was to write it himself. The same went for the priest and the same for the Levite. A plan of work." But "that other man, the sinner," let God write his story. It altered his whole afternoon, because the Lord set him before "that poor wounded man, lying in the road."

I ask myself, continued the pope, "and I ask you: do we allow God to write our life story or do we want to write it ourselves? This is a matter of obedience. Are we obedient to God's word? Yes, I want to be obedient. But are you capable of listening to it, hearing it? Are you able to find God's word in our everyday story, or are you ruled by your own ideas, which don't allow the Lord's surprise to speak to you?"

"I'm sure," Pope Francis concluded, "that today at this moment all of us are saying: but that Jonah asked for it, and those two, the priest and the Levite, they were selfish. It's true that the Samaritan, the sinner, didn't run away from God!" So I hope "the Lord may give us the grace to hear his voice, which tells us: Go and do likewise."

CHOOSING THE BETTER PART

Tuesday, October 8, 2013
JON 3:1-10; LK 10:38-42

Praying means opening the door to the Lord so that he can do something about sorting us out. A priest who does his duty but doesn't open the door to the Lord risks becoming a mere "professional." During the Mass celebrated this morning, Tuesday, October 8, in St. Martha's chapel, Pope Francis focused on the value of prayer: not "parroted" prayer but prayer "from the heart," in which we "look at the Lord, listen to the Lord, ask the Lord."

The reflection was developed from the liturgical readings, taken from the book of Jonah (3:1-10) and Luke's gospel (10:38-42). In particular, referring to the gospel passage, the pope suggested Mary's attitude was the model to follow.

She was one of the two women who had offered hospitality to Jesus in their home. Mary stops to listen to the Lord and look at him, whereas Martha, her sister, busies herself with the housework.

"The word of the Lord is clear," began the pope. "Mary has chosen the better part, of prayer, contemplation of Jesus. Her sister thought she was wasting time." Mary stopped to look at the Lord like a child full of wonder, "instead of working like Martha."

Mary's attitude is the right one because, the pope explained, "she listened to the Lord and prayed from her heart." That is what "the Lord wants to tell us. Our first duty in life is to pray. Not just parroting the words, but praying from the heart." In that way we can "look at the Lord, listen to the Lord, ask the Lord. And we know that prayer works miracles."

The story told in the book of Jonah teaches us the same thing. Jonah is "stubborn," said the Holy Father, because "he didn't want to do what the Lord asked him to." Only after the Lord has saved him from the whale's belly, recalled the pope, Jonah decided: "Lord, I'll do whatever you say. And he went through the streets of Nineveh" announcing his prophecy: the city would be destroyed by God if the citizens did not change their way of life for the better. Jonah "was a 'professional' prophet," said the bishop of Rome, "and he said: in forty days Nineveh will be destroyed. He said it seriously, powerfully. And those Ninevites were frightened, so they began to pray with words, from their hearts, with their bodies. Their prayer worked a miracle."

In this story too, said Pope Francis, "we see what Jesus says to Martha: Mary has chosen the better part. Prayer works miracles, when we're faced with the problems" there are in the world. But there are also those whom the pope called "pessimists." These people "say nothing can change; life's like that.

It reminds me of a sad song from my own country which says: Let it go. We'll all meet down there in the furnace."

Of course, he stressed, it's "rather a pessimistic view of life" that leads us to ask: "Why pray? Let it go; life's like that! Let's get on. Let's just do what we can." That was Martha's attitude, explained the pope. "She kept busy but she didn't pray." And it's the way others behave like the "stubborn Jonah." These people are "the executioners." Jonah "went and prophesied, but he said in his heart: they deserve it, they deserve it; they asked for it. He prophesied but he didn't pray; he didn't ask the Lord to forgive them, he merely slammed into them." Such people, the Holy Father stressed, "think they are being so just." But in the end, as happened to Jonah, they are shown to be selfish.

For example, explained the pope, when God saved the people of Nineveh, Jonah "got angry with the Lord: but you're always like that, you always forgive!" And "we too," commented the pope. "What we do when we don't pray is shut the door in the Lord's face," so that "he can't do anything. But when we pray about a problem, or a difficult situation, a disaster, we're opening the door to the Lord, so that he comes in"; in fact he "knows how to put things right."

In conclusion, Pope Francis urged us to think of Mary, Martha's sister, who "chose the better part and shows us the way, how to open the door to the Lord." And to think of the king of Nineveh, "who wasn't a saint," and all his people: "They did horrible things. But when they prayed and fasted and opened the door to the Lord, the Lord worked the miracle of forgiveness. And let us think of Jonah, who didn't pray, who always fled from the Lord. He prophesied; perhaps he was a good 'professional'—we could say nowadays a good priest— who did his duty, but who never opened the door to the Lord in prayer. Let us ask the Lord to help us always to choose the better part."

COURAGE TO PRAY

Thursday, October 10, 2013
MAL 3:13-20B; LK 11:5-13

Our prayer must be courageous, not lukewarm, if we not only want to receive the necessary graces but above all, through our prayer to know the Lord. If we ask him, he himself will bring us his grace. This morning, Thursday, October 10, during the Mass celebrated at St. Martha's, Pope Francis spoke again of the power and courage of prayer.

The pope explained that the liturgical passage from Luke's gospel (11:5-13) speaks of the need to pray insistently, if necessary, but always to be involved in our prayer "in this parable of the persistent, importunate friend," who goes to ask his friend late at night for bread to give to an acquaintance who has just arrived at his house and to whom he has nothing to offer. "This request," he noted, "makes the friend get up from his bed and give him the bread. And Jesus speaks to us about this on another occasion: in the parable of the widow who went to the corrupt judge, who wouldn't listen to her, didn't want to listen to her. But she's so persistent, she annoys him so much, that in the end, in order not to be bothered anymore by her, the judge gives her the justice she's asking for. That makes us think about our own prayer. How do we pray? Do we pray piously, but calmly, from force of habit, or do we stand bravely before the Lord to ask for grace, to ask for what we're praying for?"

Attitude is important, because "prayer that isn't brave," said the pope, "isn't really prayer." When we pray we must have "the courage to trust that the Lord is listening to us, the courage to knock at the door. The Lord says so: anyone who asks will receive and anyone who seeks will find and anyone who knocks will have the door opened."

But, asked the Holy Father, is our prayer like that? Or do we just say, "Lord, I need this, do me a favor"? In a word, "are we involved in our prayer? Do we know how to knock at God's heart?" In reply the bishop of Rome returned to the gospel passage, at the end of which "Jesus tells us: Is there anyone among you who, if your child asks for a fish, will give a snake instead of a fish? Or if the child asks for an egg will give a scorpion? If you, then, who are evil, know how to give good gifts to your children, how much more will your heavenly Father... And we expect him to carry on saying he will give you good things. But no, he doesn't say that! He will give the Holy Spirit to those who ask for it. And that's a great thing."

For "when we pray bravely, the Lord not only gives us grace, but he also gives us himself in the grace." For "the Lord," the pope put neatly, "never sends us a grace by mail: he brings it himself; he is the grace!"

"Today," he said in conclusion, "in the prayer, the collect, we asked the Lord to give us what even prayer dare not ask for. And what is it that we daren't ask for? The Lord himself! We ask for a grace, but we daren't say: come yourself and bring it to me. We know that grace is always brought by him. Let's not make the mistake of accepting the grace and not recognizing the one who brings it to us, the one who gives it to us, who is the Lord."

How to Defeat the Devil

Friday, October 11, 2013
Jl 1:13-15, 2:1-2; Lk 11:15-26

"Please, let's not do deals with the devil," and let us take seriously the dangers that spring from his presence in the world. That is what Pope Francis urged this morning, Friday, October 11, in his homily during the Mass at St. Martha's. "The devil is present," he reminded us, "on the first page of the Bible and also on the last with God's victory over him." But he always returns with his temptations. And it's up to us "not to be naïve."

The pope commented on the episode in which Luke (11:15-26) tells us about Jesus casting out devils. The evangelist also mentions the comments of those who were present and puzzled, accusing Jesus of magic or, at most, recognizing him only as a healer of epileptics. Even today, noted the pope, "there are priests who read this passage and other passages in the gospel and say: Jesus cured someone of a psychological illness." Certainly "it's true that at that time people confused epilepsy with possession by the devil," he recognized, "but it's also true that the devil was there. And we have no right to make matters so simple," as if it were only a question of psychological illness and not possession by the devil.

Returning to the gospel, the pope noted that Jesus gives us certain criteria to recognize the devil's presence and respond. "How can we keep walking along our Christian road when we run into temptations? When does the devil come and disturb us?" he asked. The first criterion suggested in the gospel passage "is that we can't have a half-victory of Jesus over the devil." To explain this the Holy Father quoted Jesus' words in Luke: "You are either with me or against me; anyone who isn't with me is against me and anyone who doesn't gather with me scatters." And referring to Jesus' action toward those possessed by the devil, he said that this was just a small part "of what Jesus came to do for all humanity": destroy the devil's work to free us from slavery to him.

We can't go on thinking this is an exaggeration: "Either you're with Jesus or against Jesus. There can be no shadow of doubt about this. It's a battle, a battle in which what's at stake is the eternal salvation of us all." There are no alternatives, even if we sometimes hear "pastoral proposals" that sound more accommodating. "No! Either you're with Jesus," repeated the bishop of Rome, "or you're against him. That's how it is. That's one of the criteria."

The final criterion is watchfulness. "We must always be on the watch, on the watch against the deceits, the lures of the evil one," urged the pope. And again he quoted the gospel: "When a strong man, fully armed, guards his castle, his property is safe. And we can ask ourselves the question: do I keep watch over myself? Over my heart? Over my feelings? Over my thoughts? Do I guard the treasure of grace? Do I guard the presence of the Holy Spirit in me?" If it isn't guarded, he added, again quoting the gospel, "someone stronger attacks him and overpowers him and takes away the armor in which he trusted and divides his plunder."

So these are the criteria with which to respond to the challenges we face from the presence of the devil in the world: the certainty that "Jesus fights the devil"; "anyone who isn't with Jesus is against Jesus"; and "keep watch." We must remember, said the pope, that "the devil is cunning: he is never driven away permanently; that will only happen on the last day." For, he reminded us, quoting the gospel: "when the unclean spirit has gone out of someone it wanders through waterless regions looking for a resting place, but not finding any, it says: 'I will return to my house from which I came.' When it comes it finds it swept and tidy. Then it goes and brings seven other spirits more evil than itself, and they enter and live there; and the last state of that person is worse than the first."

That's why it's necessary to keep watch. "The devil's strategy is this," said Pope Francis: "you have become a Christian, you are progressing in your faith and I leave you alone. But then when you've gotten used to that and are not very vigilant because you feel secure, I'll return. The gospel for today begins with the devil cast out and ends with the devil coming back. St. Peter said it: the devil is like a roaring lion pacing round us." And these are not lies: "it's the word of the Lord."

"Let us ask the Lord," was the pope's concluding prayer, "for the grace to take these things seriously. He came to fight for our salvation; he has overcome the devil."

THE JONAH SYNDROME

Monday, October 14, 2013
Rom 1:1-7; Lk 11:29-31

A serious illness threatening Christians today is the "Jonah syndrome," which makes you feel perfectly clean as if straight from the dry cleaners, unlike those whom we judge to be sinners and therefore condemned to fend for themselves, without any help from us. But Jesus reminds us that in order to be saved we need "the sign of Jonah," that is, the Lords' mercy. That was, in a nutshell, Pope Francis' reflection during the Mass celebrated this morning, Monday, October 14, in St. Martha's chapel.

Commenting on the liturgical readings for the day, taken from Paul's letter to the Romans (1:1-7) and Luke's gospel (11:29-32), the pope began from the "strong words" addressed by Jesus to a group of people when he called them "an evil generation." "It sounds like an insult," he noted, "to say this is an evil generation. Strong words! Jesus, who is so kind, so humble, so gentle, says these words." But, explained the pope, he certainly wasn't referring to the people following him. Instead, he was referring to the doctors of the law, who were trying to put him to the test, make him fall into a trap. They were demanding a sign from him, proofs. And Jesus replies that the only sign to be given to them will be "the sign of Jonah."

But what is the sign of Jonah? "Last week," the pope recalled, "the liturgy invited us to reflect upon Jonah. And now Jesus promises the sign of Jonah." Before explaining this sign, Pope Francis invited us to reflect on another detail in the gospel story: "the Jonah syndrome," which the prophet had in his heart. The pope explained, "he didn't want to go to Nineveh and ran away to Spain." He thought his ideas were clear. "The doctrine is this, we must believe this. If they're sinners they'll have to sort it out for themselves; it's nothing to do with me! That's the Jonah syndrome!" And "Jesus condemns it. For example, in Matthew chapter 23 those who believe in this syndrome are called hypocrites. They don't want the poor people to be saved. God says to Jonah: poor people, who can't tell right from left, they're ignorant, sinners. But Jonah continues to insist: they need justice! I keep all the commandments; let them sort it out for themselves."

That's the Jonah syndrome, which "hits those who have no desire for people to be converted; they seek holiness—let me put it this way—a holiness from the dry cleaners, that means everything fine and dandy, everything done well but without the fervor that pushes us to preach the Lord." The pope recalled that "to this people who were suffering from the Jonah syndrome the Lord promised the sign of Jonah." And he added: "The other version, in Matthew, tells us: Jonah was three nights and three days in the whale's belly... The reference is to Jesus in the tomb, to his death and resurrection. That's the sign Jesus promises: against hypocrisy, against that attitude of self-satisfied religiosity, against the attitude of a group of Pharisees."

To make it clearer, the bishop of Rome referred to another parable in the gospel "that expresses very well what Jesus means.

It's the parable of the Pharisee and the publican, who are praying in the temple (Luke 14:10-14). The Pharisee is so self-satisfied as he stands before the altar that he says: I thank you God that I am not like all those people of Nineveh or like that man over there! And that man was the publican, who only said: Lord be merciful to me, a sinner."

The sign that Jesus promises "is his forgiveness," explained Pope Francis, "through his death and resurrection. The sign that Jesus promises is his mercy, which God had already been demanding for a long time: I desire mercy and not sacrifice." So "the true sign of Jonah is that which enables us to trust that we have been saved by Christ's blood. So many Christians think they have been saved only by what they do, through their own good works. Good works are necessary but they are a consequence, a response to that merciful love that saves us." Works alone, without that merciful love, are not enough.

So "the Jonah syndrome strikes those who trust only in their own personal righteousness, in their own good works." And when Jesus says "this evil generation" he is referring "to all those who are suffering from the Jonah syndrome." But there's more: "The Jonah syndrome," said the pope, "leads us to hypocrisy, to that self-sufficiency we think we can attain because we're good, clean Christians, because we do those good works, keep the commandments, all that. It's a serious disease, the Jonah syndrome!" Whereas "the sign of Jonah" is "God's mercy in Jesus Christ who died and rose again for us, for our salvation."

"There are two words in the first reading," he added, "that connect with this. Paul says of himself that he is an apostle, not because he has studied, but because he was called to be an apostle; he says to Christians: you are called by Jesus Christ. The sign of Jonah calls us." Today's liturgy, concluded the pope, helps us to understand and to make a choice: "Do we want to go with the Jonah syndrome or the sign of Jonah?"

Loving God and Our Neighbor Against Idolatry and Hypocrisy

Tuesday, October 15, 2013
Rom 1:16-25; Lk 11:37-41

Hypocrisy and idolatry "are grievous sins," which have historical origins but also frequently occur today, even among Christians. To overcome them "is so difficult": in order to do so "we need God's grace." That was Pope Francis' reflection suggested by the readings at the Mass celebrated this morning, Tuesday, October 15, in St. Martha's chapel.

"The Lord," he began, "told us that the first commandment is to worship God, to love God. The second is to love our neighbor as ourselves. Today's liturgy speaks to us about two vices against these commandments," which in fact, he noted, are just a single commandment: to love God and our neighbor. And the vices mentioned "are grievous sins: idolatry and hypocrisy." The apostle Paul, noted the pope, does not mince his words when he is describing idolatry. He is "fiery" and "strong," and he says: "The wrath of God is revealed from heaven against all impiety and wickedness, because idolatry is impiety, it's a lack of pietas. It's a lack of that sense of worshiping God that we all have within us. And God's wrath is revealed against all impiety, against those who suffocate the truth in injustice." They suffocate the truth of faith, that faith "which was given to us in Jesus Christ, in whom God's justice is revealed." And, the pope continued, as a way from faith to faith "as John often said: grace upon grace, from faith to faith. The way of faith." But "we all need to worship, because we have God's imprint within us," and "when we don't worship God we worship creatures" and that means "turning from faith to idolatry."

Idolaters "have no excuse. For although they knew God," the bishop of Rome stressed, "they did not honor him, they did not thank him as God." But what is the way of idolaters? Paul tells the Romans very clearly: It's the way to get lost. "They became lost in their futile thinking and their senseless minds were darkened." It's "the egoism of our own thoughts, our omnipotent thoughts," that leads to this. These tell us: "what I think is true; I think the truth, I do the truth in my thinking." And claiming to be wise the people Paul is talking about "became fools, and exchanged the glory of the immortal God for images resembling a mortal human being or birds, or four-footed animals or reptiles."

We might be led to think, the pope warned, that these attitudes are in the past. "Today none of us goes about worshiping statues." But it's not like that because "even today," said the pope, "there are so many idols and even today there are so many idolaters. So many who think themselves wise, even among us Christians." And he added immediately, "I'm not talking about those who are not Christians; I respect them. But we're talking among ourselves within the family." In fact many Christians "think they are wise, that they know everything," but in the end "they become fools and exchange the glory of the immortal God for an image: their own ego," their own ideas, their own comfort.

That isn't something which just happened in the past, because "even today," said the pope, "there are idols along the way." But, he added, there's more: "All of us have a hidden idol within us. And we may ask ourselves before God: what is my hidden idol that occupies the Lord's place? A French writer, a very religious man, often became angry. It was his shortcoming; he got angry easily and often. He said: anyone who doesn't pray to God prays to the devil. If you don't worship God, you always worship an idol." Our need to worship, our need for God, arises from the fact that we bear his "imprint" within us and so "if we don't worship the living God, we will worship these idols." And concluding, almost provocatively, the pope asked us all to make an examination of conscience and ask ourselves: "What is my idol?"

The other sin "against the first commandment, propounded in today's liturgy, is hypocrisy," the Holy Father continued. The cue for this further reflection came from Luke's story in which we hear of "that man who invited Jesus to dinner and was scandalized because he didn't wash his hands." So he thought Jesus was "unrighteous" because "he didn't do what ought to be done."

But, "just as Paul doesn't mince his words against idolaters," noted the Holy Father, "Jesus doesn't mince his words against hypocrites: you Pharisees clean the outside of the cup and the plate, but inside you are full of greed and wickedness. It's very clear! You're greedy, bad, and foolish." He uses "the same word that Paul uses for idolaters: they became fools, fools. And what advice does Jesus give? So give for alms those things that are within and then everything will be cleaner for you."

So Jesus advises "not to go by appearances" but to go to the heart of the truth: "The plate is the plate but what's more important is what is on the plate: the food. But if you're vain, if you're a careerist, if you're ambitious, if you're a person who is always boasting about yourself, or who loves boasting because you think you're perfect, give alms and that will cure your hypocrisy."

"That," the pope concluded, "is the Lord's way: worship God, love God above all, and love your neighbor. It's so simple, but so difficult. We can only do it through grace. Let us ask for grace."

DISCIPLES OF CHRIST, NOT OF IDEOLOGY

Thursday, October 17, 2013
ROM 3:21-30; LK 11:47-54

"When Christians become disciples of ideology, they have lost faith and are no longer disciples of Jesus."

The only remedy for that danger is prayer. That was the message Pope Francis took from the liturgy of the word during the Mass celebrated this morning, Thursday, October 17, at St. Martha's.

The pope focused his homily on the gospel passage from Luke (11:47-54), which tells of Jesus' warning to the doctors of the law: "Woe to you who have taken away the key of knowledge; you did not enter yourselves and you hindered those who were entering." He compared it to the image of "a closed church," which "the people passing by it can't enter" and from which "the Lord who is inside can't go out." Hence the warning to "those Christians who have the key in their hands, but take it away and don't open the door," or worse, "lock the door" and "don't let anyone in."

But what's the cause of all this? The Holy Father called it "lack of Christian witness," which is even more serious if the Christian in question "is a priest, a bishop, a pope." For Jesus is very clear when he says: "Go out to the ends of the earth. Teach what I've taught you. Baptize, go to the crossroads and bring everyone in, good and bad. That's what Jesus says. Everyone in!"

According to the pope, the Christian with this "pocketed key and locked door" attitude undergoes "a spiritual and mental process" that "distills" the faith into "an ideology." But, he warned, "ideology doesn't draw people. In ideology there is no Jesus. Jesus is tenderness, love, gentleness, and any ideology is always rigid." So ideologies risk making the Christian "a disciple of that way of thinking" rather than "a disciple of Jesus."

So Jesus' rebuke still holds today: "You have taken away the key of knowledge," since "knowledge of Jesus has become ideological and moralistic knowledge." That's the way those doctors of the law behaved who "shut the door with so many rules and regulations." The pope recalled another warning by Christ—which comes in Matthew 23—against scribes and Pharisees "who lay heavy burdens on people's shoulders." And those attitudes trigger a process by which "faith becomes ideology and ideology frightens people! Ideology drives people away and distances the church from people."

Pope Francis said that "these ideological Christians have a serious disease" but he was aware as he said so that "this isn't a new disease." The apostle John spoke about it in his first letter, describing "Christians who lose faith and prefer ideologies"; they become "rigid, moralizing ethicists without kindness."

We may well ask what it is that gives rise to this kind of attitude "in the hearts of that Christian, that priest, that bishop, that pope. For Pope Francis the answer is simple: "That Christian doesn't pray and when there is no prayer" the door closes.

So "the key that opens the door to faith is prayer." Because "when Christians don't pray they become arrogant." They become "arrogant, proud people, sure of themselves, rather than humble. They seek to promote themselves. But when Christians pray they don't distance themselves from the faith; they talk with Jesus."

The Holy Father made the point that the verb "to pray" doesn't mean "to say prayers," because even the doctors of the law "said so many prayers" but only "in order to be seen." In fact, "it's one thing to pray and quite another to say prayers." In the latter case, faith is abandoned and becomes "a moralistic ideology" that is "without Jesus."

Those who pray like the doctors of the law, according to the pope, react in the same way "when a prophet or a good Christian rebukes them." They use the same means as those that were used against Jesus. "When he went out of there the scribes and Pharisees began to be very hostile to him," he said, quoting the words of the gospel passage, "and to cross-examine him about many things, setting traps for him." They wanted to catch him out "in words from his own mouth." Because, commented the pope, "these ideologists are hostile and cunning!

They aren't transparent! And the poor creatures are stained with pride!"

Hence his concluding invitation to ask the Lord for the grace never to cease "praying not to lose faith" and to "remain humble" so that we don't become closed up people, "who shut off the way of the Lord."

The Apostle's Sunset

Friday, October 18, 2013
2 Tim 4:10-17b; Lk 10:1-9

Pope Francis spoke of a strange pilgrimage during the Mass celebrated this morning, Friday, October 18, at St. Martha's. It was the visit to the retirement homes for old priests and nuns. These really are "sanctuaries of apostolic holiness," said the bishop of Rome, "that we have in the church," which are worth visiting "as a pilgrimage." That was the point of his reflection, which took its cue from the comparison between the liturgical readings for the day: the passage from Luke's gospel (10:1-9)—in which we hear about "the beginning of apostolic life" when the disciples were called and were "young, strong, and cheerful"—and Paul's second letter to Timothy (4:10-17), in which the apostle, who is now nearing "the sunset of his life," speaks about "the end of apostolic life." From this comparison we see, explained the pope, that every apostle "has a joyful, enthusiastic beginning, with God within him; but none is spared the end." And he added, "it does me good to think of the apostle's sunset."

He then went on to think about "three images": Moses, John the Baptist, and Paul. Moses is "that brave leader of God's people who fought against enemies and also battled with God to save the people. He is strong but at the end he is left alone on Mount Nebo looking towards the promised land," which he can't ever enter. Neither was John the Baptist "spared from suffering at the end of his life." He wonders whether he has made a mistake, if he has taken the right road, and sends his friends to ask Jesus, "Are you the one or should we wait for another?" He is tormented with anguish, so that "this greatest man born of woman," as Christ himself calls him, ends up "in the power of a weak, drunken, and corrupt governor, who is prey to an envious adulteress and subject to a dancer's whim."

Finally, Paul confesses all his bitterness to Timothy. To describe his sufferings the bishop of Rome used the expression "he's not in the seventh heaven." And he quoted the apostle's words: "My son, do your best to come to me soon, for Demas, in love with the present world, has deserted me and gone to Thessalonica. Crescens has gone to Galatia, Titus to Dalmatia. Only Luke is with me. Get Mark and bring him with you, for he is useful in my ministry... Bring the cloak I left, also the books and above all the parchments. Alexander the coppersmith did me great harm... You also must beware of him, for he strongly opposed our message." The pope then recalled Paul's account of his trial: "At my first defense no one came to my support, but all deserted me ... but the Lord stood by me and gave me strength, so that through me the message might be fully proclaimed." According to the pope this image shows the "sunset" of every apostle: "alone, abandoned, betrayed"; helped only by the Lord who "doesn't abandon, doesn't betray," because "he is faithful; he can't go back on his word."

The apostle's greatness, the pope stressed, lies in making his life accord with what John the Baptist said: "He must increase and I must decrease." The apostle is one "who gives his life for the Lord to increase. And at the end comes his sunset." It was like that for Peter, said Pope Francis. Jesus had predicted: "when you are old, they will take you where you don't want to go."

His meditation on the final stages of these people's lives reminded the Holy Father of "those sanctuaries of apostolic holiness that are the retirement homes for priests and nuns." They house "good priests and nuns who have grown old, who suffer loneliness, waiting for the Lord to come and knock at the door of their heart." Unfortunately, said the pope, we tend to forget about these sanctuaries: "They aren't beautiful places because we see what's to come for us." However, "if we look more deeply, they are very beautiful," because of the human richness they contain. To visit them is "a real pilgrimage, to these sanctuaries of apostolic holiness," like pilgrimages made to the shrines of Our Lady or the saints.

But I wonder, added the pope, do we Christians want to pay a visit—which would be a real pilgrimage!—to these sanctuaries of apostolic holiness that these retirement homes for priests and nuns are? One of you told me the other day that when he went to a mission country, he went to the cemetery and saw all the graves of the old missionaries, the priests and nuns, buried there for 50, 100, 200 years, unknown. And he said to me, 'But all these could be canonized because at the end of the day what counts is that daily holiness, that everyday holiness.'"

In these retirement homes, said the pope, "the nuns and priests are awaiting the Lord rather like Paul: actually, rather sad, but also with a kind of peace, with happy faces." For that very reason, it "does all of us good to think about that stage of life which is the apostle's sunset." And in conclusion, he asked us to pray to the Lord to keep the priests and nuns who are at the final stage of their lives, so that they can repeat just once more: "Yes, Lord, I want to follow you."

MONEY IS USEFUL BUT GREED KILLS

Monday, October 21, 2013
ROM 4:20-25; LK 12:13-21

Money is useful for many good works, to promote human progress, but when it becomes the only thing in life it destroys us and our relationships with other people. That was the teaching Pope Francis took from the reading from Luke's gospel (12:13-21) in this morning's liturgy, on Monday, October 21, at St. Martha's.

At the beginning of his homily the Holy Father recalled the man who asks Jesus to tell his brother to divide the inheritance with him. Indeed, for the pope, the Lord speaks to us through this character "of our relationship with wealth and money." That is not just a subject for two thousand years ago, but one which arises constantly today, every day. "How many families," he remarked, "have we seen destroyed by money problems: brother against brother, father against children!" For the first result of attachment to money is that it destroys a person and those around them around. "When someone is attached to money," explained the bishop of Rome, "they destroy themselves and their family."

Of course we shouldn't demonize money absolutely. "Money can bring about many good things," Pope Francis pointed out, "so many achievements to develop humanity." But what is wrong is using it perversely. Here the pope quoted the very words used by Jesus in the gospel parable of the "rich man." "Those who store up treasures for themselves are not rich towards God." Hence the warning. "Take care! Be on your guard against all kinds of greed." And this is what "does harm in our relationship to money"; it's the constant temptation to want more that "leads to idolatry" of money and ends up destroying "our relationships with other people." For greed makes us sick, it leads to a vicious circle in which our every single thought is "about money."

What's more, greed's most dangerous characteristic is that it "leads to idolatry; because it goes the opposite way" to the way laid out for us by God. Here the Holy Father quoted St. Paul, who said, "Jesus Christ, who was rich, became poor in order to enrich us." So it's "God's way," the way of "humility, lowering ourselves in order to serve." Greed and idolatry lead us in the opposite direction: "You, who are a poor human being, make yourself out to be God through vanity."

That's why, added the pope, "Jesus says such strong, harsh words against attachment to money." For example, when he says: "You cannot serve two masters: you must serve either God or money." Or when he urges us "not to be worried because the Lord knows what we need." Or again when he tells us to "trust in the Father, who makes the lilies of the field bloom and gives food to the birds of heaven."

That attitude of trust in the divine mercy is the very opposite of the attitude of the man in the gospel parable. He only thinks of the abundant harvest his land has produced and the crops he has gathered. When he was wondering what to do with them, explained Pope Francis, "he could have said: I'll give to someone else to help him." Instead, "his greed led him to say: I'll build larger barns and fill them. More and more." Such behavior, according to the pope, shows an ambition to attain a sort of divinity, "an almost idolatrous divinity," as the man's own words show: "Soul, you have ample goods laid up for many years. Eat, drink, and be merry."

But it's at that very moment that God brings him back to his reality as a creature. He warns him saying: "You fool! This very night your life will be demanded of you." For, the bishop of Rome concluded, "the way that leads in the opposite direction to God's way is foolishness; it leads away from life. It destroys all human kindness." But the Lord shows us the right way. Which "isn't the way of poverty for poverty's sake." On the contrary, "it's the way of poverty as an instrument, so that God may be God, so that he may be the only Lord, not the golden idol." Indeed, "all the goods we have are given to us by the Lord to help the world go forward, to help humanity go forward, to help others."

So the pope prayed that "the Lord's word may remain in our hearts today" with his invitation to keep away from greed, because "even if we have in abundance, our lives don't depend on what we possess."

MIND, HEART, CONTEMPLATION

Tuesday, October 22, 2013
ROM 5:12, 15B, 17, 19, 20B-21; LK 12:35-38

God didn't save us by decree or by law, he saved us with his life. This is a mystery, which we can't understand by our mind alone. So if we try to explain it only with our mind it may drive us mad. In order to understand it, said Pope Francis in his homily during the Mass celebrated on Tuesday morning, October 22, at St. Martha's, we need something else.

Naturally, this is something that it isn't easy to grasp or explain. "The passage from the letter to the Romans we heard in the first reading—said the pope, quoting some passages from chapter 5 of the letter (vv. 12, 15, 17-19, 20-21)—may be one of the most difficult. We can see that poor Paul is having trouble proclaiming this, in order to make it understood." Nevertheless, he helps us get closer to the truth. And the Holy Father gave us three words that can help our understanding: contemplation, closeness, and abundance.

First, contemplation. Of course, said the pope, we're talking about an extraordinary mystery, so great that "when the church wants to tell us something about this mystery she just uses the word 'wonderfully.' She says: God 'who wonderfully created the world and even more wonderfully re-created it...'" Paul wants us to understand this: to understand it we need to kneel down and pray and contemplate. "Contemplation is mind, heart, knees, prayer"; and putting all of them together, said the bishop of Rome, means entering the mystery. So what Paul is telling us about salvation and the redemption wrought by Jesus "can only be understood on our knees, in contemplation, not with the mind alone." For "when the mind tries to explain a mystery, it always drives us mad. That has happened during the church's history."

The pope's second word was "closeness," an idea, he noted, that often occurs in our passage. "One man committed the sin, another man has saved us. He is the God who is close to us. This mystery shows us a God who is close to us, to our history. From the first moment when he chose our father Abraham, he walked with his people, he sent his son to do this work."

A work that Jesus does like a craftsman, a workman. The pope confided that "the image that comes to my mind is of a nurse, working in a hospital who cures wounds one by one, but with her own hands. God becomes involved in our troubles; he comes close to our wounds and cures them with his own hands. And in order to have hands he became man. It's Jesus' own personal work. A man committed the sin, a man comes to cure it." For "God doesn't save us just by a decree, or a law; he saves us with tenderness, with his caresses; he saves us with his life for us."

The pope's third word was "abundance." It's repeated several times in Paul's letter: "But where sin was abundant, grace was superabundant." That sin abounds in the world and in each of our hearts is obvious: "Each of us knows our troubles, knows them well. They are abundant. But God's challenge is to conquer sin, cure its wounds, as Jesus did." And what's more "to give us the superabundant gift of his love and his grace."

Hence we can understand Jesus' "preference for sinners. He was accused of eating with publicans and sinners. Eating with publicans was a scandal, because sin abounded in such people's hearts. But he went to them with that superabundance of grace and love." And God's grace, the pope explained, "always conquers, because it is himself he gives, who comes close, caresses us, heals us."

Of course, the pope stressed, we don't like hearing that sinners are closer to Jesus' heart, that "he goes out to seek them, calls them all: come, come… And when asked for an explanation he says: those who are well don't need a physician; I came to heal, to save abundantly."

In conclusion Pope Francis recalled, some saints "say that one of the worst sins is distrust, distrust of God. But how can we distrust a God who is so close to us, so kind, who prefers our sinful heart? And that's the mystery; it's not easy to understand it, it can't easily be grasped, it can't be understood by our minds alone. Perhaps these three words will help us: contemplation, contemplating the mystery; closeness, the mystery, hidden for centuries, of a God who is near, who comes close to us; and abundance, a God who always conquers by the superabundance of his grace, by his tenderness or, as we heard in the collect, with the wealth of his mercy."

The Logic of Before and After

Thursday, October 24, 2013
Rom 6:19-23; Lk 12:49-53

We need to follow "the logic of before and after" so that we don't become "lukewarm Christians" or "watered down"

Christians, even if not actual hypocrites. During the Mass celebrated on Thursday morning, October 24, in St. Martha's chapel,
Pope Francis used this telling expression to return to the attitude
with which Christians should approach the mystery of salvation
brought about by Jesus.

He began by referring to the letter to the Romans (6:19-
23), in which St. Paul "tries to make us understand that great
mystery of our redemption, our forgiveness, the forgiveness
of our sins in Christ Jesus." The apostle tells us that it isn't
easy to understand and really feel this mystery. To help us
understand it he uses what the pope defined as "the logic of
before and after: before Jesus and after Jesus," summed up in
the gospel acclamation in the day's liturgy (Philippians 3:8):
"For his sake I have suffered the loss of all things, and regard
them as rubbish, in order that I may gain Christ and be found
in him." So for St. Paul, only Christ counts. "He felt it so
strongly," said the pope, "the faith that makes us righteous,
that justifies us before the Father." Paul has abandoned his
"before" self. And he has become his "after" self, whose aim is
to "win Christ."

Continuing with his commentary on the letter, the Holy Father noted how the apostle points out "a way to live according
to this logic of before and after." A way described in the words:
"For just as you once presented your members as slaves to impu-
rity and to greater and greater iniquity, so now you present your
members as slaves to uprightness, for sanctification."

"What Christ did in us," said the pope, "was a re-creation.
Christ's blood has re-created us; it's a second creation. And if
before, our whole life, our whole body, our whole soul, all our
habits were on the road of sin, of iniquity, after this re-creation
we must make the effort to walk the way of uprightness, of
sanctification. Paul uses this word: holiness. We have all been
baptized. At that time—we were babies—our parents declared

the act of faith in our name: I believe in Jesus Christ who has forgiven our sins."

"We have to take up this faith again," urged the pope, "and carry it forward in our way of life. Living as a Christian means carrying on this faith in Christ, this re-creation. Carrying on the works that arise from that faith. The important thing is faith, but works are the fruit of this faith: carrying on these works for sanctification. So: the first sanctification that was Christ's work, the first sanctification that we received in baptism must grow, must advance."

Actually, admitted the Holy Father, "we're weak and we often commit sins." Does that mean we're not on the way to sanctification? "Yes and no," Pope Francis answered. And he explained: "If you become accustomed to a so-so life and say, 'I believe in Jesus Christ, but I'll live as I please,'" then "that doesn't sanctify you; it won't do, it's nonsense." But "if you say, 'Yes, I'm a sinner, I'm weak,'" and "you always go to the Lord and say, 'Lord, you've got the strength, give me faith; you can heal me,'" through the sacrament of reconciliation, then "even our imperfections become part of this way of sanctification."

So there is always that before and after: "First, the act of faith. Before we were accepted by Jesus Christ who re-created us with his blood, we were on the way of unrighteousness; afterwards, we're on the way of sanctification, but we have to take it seriously. That means, the pope said, doing "works of righteousness." Above all, worship God; and then "do what Jesus advises us: help one another, give food to the hungry, drink to the thirsty, visit the sick, visit prisoners. These works are works which Jesus did during his lifetime, works of righteousness, works of re-creation. When we give the hungry something to eat, we re-create hope in them and so it is with the other works. But if we don't accept the faith and don't live by it, our Christianity is just a memory: yes, I was baptized; that's the faith of my baptism, but I live as I can."

Without this awareness of before and after, "our Christianity's no good to anyone." So it becomes "hypocrisy: I say I'm a Christian but I live as a pagan. Sometimes we call this being halfway Christians," who don't seriously consider that they have been "sanctified by Christ's blood." And if we don't take that sanctification seriously we become like those the pope called "lukewarm Christians: yes yes, no no… A bit like what our mothers called watered down Christians: so-so Christians, a varnish of Christianity, a varnish of catechism, but inside there isn't real conversion, there isn't that burning conviction St. Paul had: I have suffered the loss of all things, and regard them as rubbish, in order that I may gain Christ and be found in him."

"That was Paul's passion," said the bishop of Rome. And that should be "a Christian's passion: to let go of everything that distances us from Christ the Lord; to let go of everything that distances us from the act of faith in him, the act of faith in our re-creation through his blood. And making all things new in Christ. In Christ all things are made new. Everything is new."

Is that aim possible? "Yes," answered the pope, explaining: "Paul did it. So many Christians have done it and are doing it. Not just the saints, the ones we know. There are also unknown saints, those who take their Christianity seriously. Perhaps the question we should ask ourselves today is: 'Do I want to take my Christianity seriously? Do I believe that I've been re-created by Christ's blood and do I want to carry on this re-creation to the day in which the new city, the new creation will appear? Or am I a halfway Christian?'"

"Let us ask St. Paul, who speaks to us today about this logic of before and after," the pope concluded, "to give us the grace to live seriously as Christians, to truly believe we've been sanctified by the blood of Jesus Christ."

ABLE TO BE ASHAMED

Friday, October 25, 2013
ROM 7:18-25A; LK 12:54-59

The grace of shame is what we experience when we confess our sin to God and do so speaking "face to face" with the priest, "our brother." Rather than deciding to approach God directly, as if we were "confessing by email." With this striking expression Pope Francis focused attention on one of the cardinal sacraments for human salvation, confession. He spoke about it this morning, Friday, October 25, during the Mass celebrated in St. Martha's chapel.

After having felt what it was to be liberated by Christ's blood—"re-created"—St. Paul realizes that there is still something in himself that keeps him enslaved. And in the passage from the letter to the Romans (7:18-25) read in the liturgy of the day, the pope recalled, the apostle calls himself "unhappy." "Yesterday Paul spoke about, proclaimed, salvation in Jesus Christ through faith," whereas today "speaking as their brother, he tells his brothers and sisters in Rome about the struggle he has with himself: 'For I know that nothing good dwells within me, that is, in my flesh. I can will what is right, but I cannot do it. For I do not do the good I want, but the evil that I do not want is what I do. Now if I do what I do not want, it is no longer I that do it, but sin that dwells within me.' He confesses he is a sinner. He tells us: 'Christ has saved us, we are free. But I am a poor wretch, I am a sinner, I am a slave.'"

He's talking about what the pope called "the Christian struggle," our everyday struggle. "When I want to do good," explained the pope, "sin is there beside me! Indeed deep within me. I agree to God's law, but in my members I see another law that fights against the law of my reason and enslaves me."

And we don't always have the courage to speak like Paul about this struggle. We're always seeking a justification: 'But we're all sinners.'"

We must fight against this attitude. And "if we don't realize this," the Holy Father warned, "we can't have God's forgiveness, because if being a sinner is just a word, a way of speaking, we don't need God's forgiveness. But if what enslaves us is a reality, we need the Lord's inner liberation, we need that strength." And Paul tells us the way out: "He confesses his sin, his tendency to sin, to the community; he doesn't hide it. That's the attitude the church demands of all of us, that Jesus asks of all of us: to humbly confess our sins."

In her wisdom the church offers believers the sacrament of reconciliation. And we're called to do this, insisted the pope: "Let us go to our brother, our brother the priest, and make our inner confession to him: just as Paul does: 'I want the good, I'd like to be better but, you know, sometimes I have this struggle, sometimes I have this and this and this…'" And just as "the salvation Jesus brings us is so real and particular, so are our sins."

The pope then referred to those who refused to go to the priest and maintained that they confessed directly to God. Of course, he commented, "it's easy, it's like confessing by email… God's there, far away. I say things but it's not face to face, it's not a meeting eye to eye." But "Paul confesses his weakness to his brothers face to face."

The pope also rebuked those who went to the priest but "confessed such airy-fairy things, with no particulars." Confessing like that "might just as well be not at all," he insisted. And he added. "Confessing our sins isn't a session with a psychiatrist, or a torture session. It's telling the Lord: 'Lord, I'm a sinner.' But saying it through your brother, to make it more actual and particular: 'I'm a sinner for this and this and this.'"

The pope then said he admired the way children confess.

"Today," he explained, "we heard in the alleluia: 'I thank you, Father, Lord of heaven and earth, because you revealed the mysteries of the kingdom to little ones' (Matthew 11:25). Children have a kind of wisdom. When children go to confession they never say general things, but: 'Father, I did this, I did this to my aunt, I did that to someone else, I said this word,' and they say what the word was. They give particulars, they have the simplicity of truth. But we always have the tendency to hide the reality of our misdeeds." But "when we confess our sins as they are in God's presence," that is much better. "We always feel that grace of shame. Being ashamed before God is a grace. It's a grace: 'I'm ashamed.' Think of what Peter said to Jesus after the miracle on the lake: 'Go away from me, Lord, I'm a sinner.' He felt ashamed of his sin in the presence of Jesus Christ's holiness."

Going to confession "is going to meet the Lord, who forgives us, who loves us. And what we offer him is our shame: 'Lord, I'm a sinner, but look I'm not that bad; I'm able to be ashamed.'" So, the pope concluded, "let us ask for this grace to live truthfully without hiding anything from God and without hiding anything from ourselves."

A SPECIAL DAY

Monday, October 28, 2013
EPH 2:19-22; LK 6:12-19

It's good to pray for one another. During the Mass celebrated in St. Martha's chapel this morning, Monday, October 28, Pope Francis dwelt on the value of prayer for our neighbor who is going through a difficult time.

The pope's reflection began with a comment on the gospel passage from Luke (6:12-19), which relates Jesus' choosing of the twelve apostles. It's a special day, he said, "because it's the day the apostles were chosen." And Jesus chooses them only after he has prayed to the Father "on his own."

Indeed, when Jesus prays the Father is alone with him. Then Jesus rejoins his disciples and chooses the twelve, whom he calls apostles. After that he goes with them among the people who were waiting to be healed by him. These are the three moments of the day: Jesus who spends "a whole night praying to the Father" on the mountain; Jesus among his apostles; Jesus among the people. And at the heart of all these three moments, the pope explained, is prayer: Jesus prays to the Father because he is "intimate" with him; he prays to him "for the people who come to find him"; and he also prays to him "for the apostles."

To help us better understand the meaning of Jesus' payer, the bishop of Rome also recalled "that beautiful speech after supper on Holy Thursday, when Jesus prayed to the Father saying: I pray for these, my own; but then I pray for everybody, so that they too may come and believe."

Jesus' prayer "is a universal prayer" but it's also "a personal prayer." It wasn't by accident, the pope recalled, that "on the night of that same day he looked at Peter who was acting brave and said: Peter, Satan has been allowed to sift you like wheat; but I have prayed for you that your faith may not fail." And then he urges: "Pray for everyone to the Father." And the bishop of Rome went on immediately to add: "Today I'd like us all to look at Jesus praying."

But, asked the pope, if it's true that Jesus prayed then, does he still pray today? "Well, yes, the Bible tells us so," he replied. And he explained: "He's the intercessor, the one who prays," and he prays to the Father "with us and before us. Jesus saved us. He offered that great prayer, the sacrifice of his life to save us. We've been redeemed by him. Now he has gone away. And he prays."

So "Jesus is a person, a human being with flesh like us, but in glory. Jesus bears his wounds on his hands, his feet, his side. When he prays he shows them to the Father as the price of our redemption and he prays for us. It's as if he said: 'Father, don't let this go for nothing.'" Jesus, Pope Francis continued, always has our salvation in mind. And "that's why when we pray we say: through our Lord Jesus Christ, your son. Because he's the first to pray, he's our brother. He's human like us. Jesus is the intercessor."

The Holy Father went on to ask: after gaining our redemption and saving us, "What's he doing now? He intercedes, he prays for us," he replied. "I think," he continued, "about what Peter must have felt after he'd denied Jesus, when Jesus looked at him and he wept. He felt that what Jesus had said was true. Jesus had prayed for him and that's why he was able to weep, was able to repent."

"So often," added the pope," we say to each other: "'Pray for me,' don't we? 'I need it; I've got so many problems, so many things going on, pray for me.'" And that, he declared, "is a good thing," because "we ought to pray for one another." And he asked: "Do we say to Jesus, 'Pray for me, you who are the first among us, will you pray for me?' Of course Jesus prays, but saying 'Pray for me, Lord, you are the intercessor' shows great trust. He prays for me, he prays for all of us. And he prays bravely because he shows the Father the price of our redemption, his wounds."

"Let's think about this a lot," he said in conclusion, "and thank the Lord, thank a brother who prays with us and prays for us, intercedes for us. And let's speak to Jesus. Let's tell him: 'Lord, you are the intercessor, you have saved me, you have redeemed me, but now pray for me.' Let us entrust our problems, our life to him, so that he can take them to the Father."

HOPE THE UNKNOWN

Tuesday, October 29, 2013
ROM 8:18-25; LK 13:18-21

Hope is the humblest of the three theological virtues because it tends to hide. Nevertheless, it changes us deep within, as "a pregnant woman is a woman" but it's as if she was being changed because she is becoming a mother. Pope Francis spoke about hope this morning, Tuesday, October 29, during the Mass celebrated at St. Martha's. He reflected on the attitude of Christians awaiting the revelation of the Son of God.

Hope is bound up with this attitude. It's a virtue, the pope said at the beginning of his homily, that shows more strongly in sufferings, as Paul writes in his letter to the Romans (8:18-25). "Paul," noted the pope, "refers to the sufferings of the present time, and says they are nothing in comparison to the future glory that will be revealed in us." The apostle speaks of "ardent expectation," a tension in the whole of creation as it awaits this revelation. "That tension is hope," he said, "and living in hope means living in that state of tension," awaiting the revealing of the Son of God, that is, when all creation "and also each of us" will be freed from slavery "to enter into the glory of the children of God."

"Paul," he continued, "speaks to us of hope. He had also spoken about hope in the previous chapter of his letter to the Romans. He told us that hope doesn't deceive; it is certain." Of course, that's not easy to understand. Hope doesn't mean being optimistic. For "hope isn't optimism, it's not that ability to see everything in a cheerful light and carry on"; neither is it just a positive attitude, like that of "some sunny, positive people." "That's a good thing," said the Holy Father, "but it isn't hope."

The Holy Father explained hope is called "the humblest of the three virtues, because it tends to be hidden. Faith can be seen, felt, we know what it is; charity is something to be done, we know what that is too. But what's hope?" The pope's answer was clear: "To get a bit closer we can say first of all that it's a risk. Hope is a risky virtue, a virtue, as Paul tells us, of ardent expectation of the revelation of the Son of God. It's not an illusion. It's what the children of Israel had." For when they were freed from slavery they said: "we thought we were dreaming. Now our mouths are smiling and our tongues are filled with joy."

Yes, he explained, that's what will happen at the revelation of the Son of God. "Hoping means just that: waiting in tension for this revelation, for this joy which will fill our mouths with smiling." And he exclaimed: "What a beautiful image!" Then he explained that "the early Christians depicted it as an anchor. Hope is an anchor." It's an anchor fixed to the shore of the hereafter. Our life is like being drawn on a rope towards that anchor. "But where are we anchored?" asked the bishop of Rome. "Are we anchored there, on the shore of that faraway ocean, or are we anchored in an artificial pond made by ourselves, with our own rules, our own activities, our own timetables, our own clericalism and ecclesiastical attitudes— and we don't mean the mind of the church. Are we anchored there where everything is safe and comfy? That's not hope."

"Paul then finds another image of hope," added Pope Francis, "that of childbirth. We know that the whole creation, and we with it, 'are groaning in labor pains until now.' And not only the creation, but we ourselves who have the first fruits of the Spirit groan—think of a woman in labor—groan inwardly in expectation. We're waiting. It is like giving birth." Hope, he added, comes with this dynamic of giving life. It isn't something visible, even for those who have "the first fruits of the Spirit." But we know that "the Spirit works. The gospel," said the pope, referring to the passage from Luke (13:18-21), "says something about it. The Spirit works in us. It works as if it were a mustard seed, tiny but inside it's full of life and strength and grows into a tree. The

Spirit works like leaven, which is capable of leavening the whole lump of dough. That's how the Spirit works."

Hope "is a grace to ask for." Indeed "it's one thing to live in hope, because in hope we are saved, and another to live like good Christians and nothing more: to live in expectation of the revelation or live well according to the commandments." To be anchored on the shore of the world to come "or parked on an artificial pond."

To explain the idea better the pope described the change in Mary, "a young girl." When she learns she is going to be a mother, "she goes to help and sings a song of praise." Because, Pope Francis explained, "when a woman is pregnant, she's a woman" but it's as if she was being changed deep within herself because now "she's a mother." And hope is rather like that: "it changes our attitude." So, he added, "let us ask for the grace to be men and women of hope."

In conclusion, the pope turned to a group of Mexican priests, who were celebrating the twenty-fifth anniversary of their priesthood. He pointed to the image of Mary they had brought with them as a gift and said: "Look at your mother, a figure of the hope of America. Look, she's shown as pregnant. She is the Madonna of America, she is the Madonna of hope. Ask her for the grace that the years to come may be years of hope," for the grace "to live as priests of hope," who give hope.

Pontifical Mass at the Tomb of John Paul II in St. Sebastian's Chapel in the Vatican Basilica

Two Images and a Question

Thursday, October 31, 2013

More than a hundred and twenty priests concelebrated with the Holy Father. Most of them were Polish and they included the Papal Almo-

ner Konrad Krajewski. Commenting on the day's readings, taken from the letter to the Romans (8:31-39) and Luke's gospel (13:31-35), the pope delivered the following homily.

There are two things that strike us in the readings for the day. First, Paul's certainty: "No one can separate me from the love of Christ." He loved the Lord so much—because he had seen him, he had found him, the Lord had changed his life—he loved him so much that he said nothing could separate him from the Lord. That love for the Lord was the center, the very center of Paul's life. Persecutions, sickness, betrayals, nothing that he had gone through, nothing that had happened to him in his life, could separate him from the love of Christ. It was the very center of his life, the touchstone: the love of Christ. And without the love of Christ, without living by this love, recognizing it, being nourished by this love, you can't be a Christian. A Christian is someone who feels he is being looked at by the Lord, with that beautiful look, loved by the Lord and loved to the very end. The Christian feels that his life has been saved by Christ's blood. And this gives rise to love: a loving relationship. That's the first thing that strikes me so strongly.

The other thing that strikes me is Jesus' sadness, when he looks at Jerusalem: "But you, Jerusalem, who haven't understood love." She hasn't understood God's tenderness, as Jesus expresses it in that beautiful image. Not understanding God's love. That's the opposite of what Paul felt. Yes, God loves us, but it's an abstract thing, something that doesn't touch my heart and I get on with my life as best I can. There's no faithfulness there. And Jesus weeps over Jerusalem saying this: Jerusalem, you aren't faithful; you haven't let yourself be loved; you've run after so many idols, who promised you everything, told you they would give you everything, and then forsook you." The heart of Jesus, the love Jesus suffers for: a love that isn't accepted, or welcomed.

These are the two images for today: the image of Paul who stays faithful to the end to the love of Jesus, and draws strength from it to carry on, to bear everything. He feels himself to be weak, a sinner, but finds strength in God's love, in that meeting he had with Jesus Christ. On the other hand, the unfaithful, faithless city and people, who don't accept the love of Jesus, or who are even worse than that, aren't they? They experience this love but only halfway: a bit yes, a bit no, according to what suits them. Let's look at Paul with his courage that arises from that love and let's look at Jesus weeping over that city, which is faithless. Let's look at Paul's faithfulness and the faithlessness of Jerusalem, and in the middle let's see Jesus, his heart which loves us so. What can we make of it? The question is, Am I more like Paul or Jerusalem? Is my love of God as strong as Paul's, or is my heart rather lukewarm like Jerusalem's? May the Lord, through the intercession of the Blessed John Paul, help us to answer this question. So be it!

THE PARTY INVITATION THAT CAN'T BE BOUGHT

Tuesday, November 5, 2013
ROM 12:5-16A; LK 14:15-24

"Christian life is a free invitation" to the party; the invitation can't be bought, because it comes from God. We have to answer it by taking part and sharing in it. That was the reflection suggested to Pope Francis by the liturgical readings for the day (Romans 12:5-16a; Luke 14:15-24) during the Mass celebrated this morning, Tuesday, November 5, at St. Martha's. These readings, he explained, "show us what a Christian's identity card is like, what a Christian is like." And from it we heard "first of all" that "Christian life is an invitation: we become Christians only if we're invited."

The bishop of Rome described this invitation. He said it's "a free invitation and the sender is God. But a free invitation, he warned, has consequences, the first of which is that if you haven't been invited you can't just say: 'I'll buy a ticket at the door!'" In fact, said the Holy Father, "you can't! You can't pay to get in; either you're invited or you can't go in. If we don't feel sure we've been invited, we haven't understood what being a Christian means. We're freely invited, purely by God's grace, purely by the Father's love. And it was Jesus who, through his blood, made it possible for us."

Then Pope Francis explained in more detail what the Lord's invitation means for any Christian. It's not an invitation "to go for a walk" but "to a party; to enjoy yourself; to the joy of being saved, the joy of being redeemed"; to the joy of sharing our life with Jesus. And the pope also suggested what should be understood by the term "party": "a gathering of people, speaking, laughing, enjoying themselves, being happy," he said. But the main thing is that it's a "get together" of a number of people. "Among mentally normal people I've never seen anyone who parties alone; that would be rather boring!" he explained with a joke about that sad character intent on "opening a bottle of wine" to drink a toast by himself.

So for a party we need company, to be "with others, with family and friends." In short a party "means sharing." So being a Christian implies "belonging. We belong to that group," made up of "people who've been invited to a party," a party that "brings us all together," a "feast of togetherness."

Among others things, the passage from Luke's gospel gives us "the list of those who've been invited": the poor, the crippled, the blind, the lame. "Those who have problems," stressed the pope, "who are a bit on the edge of normal city life. They will be the first at this party." But there's also room for all the others, so in Matthew's version we find more clearly: "everyone, good and bad." And from that "everyone" Pope Francis drew the conclusion that "the church isn't just for good people," but "sinners too; all we sinners have been invited" to enliven "a community that has different gifts." A community in which "everyone has a quality, a virtue," because the party happens by sharing in common with everyone else what each person has.

So "you have to take part fully." You can't just say: "I'll go to the party but I'll just say hello to three or four people I know." Because "you can't do this in the church: either you come in and be with everyone or you stay outside. You can't pick and choose."

The pope then went on to say something about God's mercy, which reaches even those who turn down the invitation or pretend to accept it but don't fully take part in the party. Once again he took his cue from Luke's passage, which lists the excuses given by some of the guests who were too busy to come. These people "take part only in name; they don't accept the invitation, they say yes," but they mean no. For Pope Francis they are the predecessors of those "Christians who are content only to be on the guest list. 'Listed' Christians." However, being "listed as a Christian isn't enough. If you don't go to the party, you aren't a Christian; you can be on the list but that doesn't bring you salvation," warned the pope.

Summing up his reflection, the pope named five things connected with "going to church" and hence "belonging to the church." First there's "grace, an invitation—you can't buy this right." Secondly, it means "being in a community, sharing all that we have—our virtues, the qualities the Lord has given us—to serve one another." Then we have to "be available for what the Lord asks of us." And that means "not asking for a special way or a special door." Lastly, it means "becoming part of the people of

God on the road to eternity," and of which "no one is a protagonist," because "we already have one who has done everything"
and only he can be "the protagonist." Hence Pope Francis urged
us all to stand "right behind him; anyone who isn't behind him is
someone making excuses." Like the people who, to paraphrase
the gospel, said: "I've bought a field, I've just got married, I've
bought some cattle, so I can't walk behind him."

Of course, said the Holy Father, "the Lord is very generous"
and "opens every door." He "also understands the one who says:
No, Lord, I don't want to come to you. He understands and waits,
because he's merciful." But he doesn't accept lies: "The Lord
doesn't like a man who says yes but whose actions say no. Who
pretends to say thank you for so many fine things, but really goes
his own way. Someone with good manners but who does what he
wants, not what the Lord wants."

So the pope's final invitation was to ask God for the grace to
understand "how lovely it is to be invited to the party, how lovely
it is to share our own qualities with everyone, how lovely it is to
be with him." And on the other hand, "how horrible it is to muck
about with yes and no, to say yes but to be content only" to be
"listed" on the guest list of Christians.

GOD DOESN'T LIKE LOSING

Thursday, November 7, 2013
ROM 14:7-12; LK 15:1-10

God is a father "who doesn't like losing." He looks with joy
and "loving weakness" for people who are lost. This often
arouses "the murmuring music of hypocrisy" in the priggish. That
was the key to today's reading suggested by Pope Francis in his

homily at the Mass celebrated on Thursday morning, November 7, in the chapel of St. Martha's House. He was commenting on the gospel passage from Luke (15:1-10).

The pope began his meditation by describing the attitude of the Pharisees and scribes, who were studying Jesus "to get what he was up to." They were scandalized "by the things he did. And as they were scandalized, they murmured against him: but this man is dangerous!" Scribes and Pharisees, explained the Holy Father, believed Jesus was a danger. That's why on Good Friday they "demanded that he should be crucified." And before that they had already come to the point of saying, "It's better for one man to die for the people so the Romans don't come in. This man is a danger!"

What scandalized them most, Pope Francis continued, was seeing Jesus "going to lunch and supper with publicans and sinners, talking with them." Hence their reaction: "This man is offending God, he's desecrating the prophetic ministry which is sacred"; and "he desecrates it by approaching such people."

"The music of this murmuring—and Jesus tells them so to their face—is the music of hypocrisy," declared the pope and said that in the gospel passage Jesus responded to "this murmuring hypocrisy with a parable." Four times in this short passage, noted the pope, "the word joy or happiness recurs: joy three times and happiness once."

In practice, said the bishop of Rome, it's as if Jesus said: "You are scandalized but my Father rejoices." That is "the deepest message: God's joy." A God "who doesn't like losing. And so as not to lose anyone, he goes out and searches for them." He is "like a shepherd" in the parable related by Luke the evangelist, "who goes out to search for the lost sheep," and even though it's dark, he leaves the other sheep "safe and goes to find the one" that's missing; "he goes to find it."

So "our God is a God who searches. His work," the pope

stressed, "is to search: to go out searching in order to invite them back. As we heard yesterday: invite all of them, good and bad." Basically, God "won't tolerate losing a single one of his own. That was also Jesus' prayer on Maundy Thursday: Father, let not one of those you have given me be lost."

So he is "a God who goes out to search for you," repeated Pope Francis, "and he has a certain loving weakness for those who are farthest away, those who are lost. He goes and looks for them. And how does he search? He searches to the end. Like that shepherd who goes out in the dark searching until he finds the lost sheep"; or like the woman who had lost a coin: she lit her lamp, swept the house, and searched all over it." God searches because he thinks: "I won't lose this child, it's my child! And I don't want to lose him!" He is "our Father. He always looks for us."

But God's "work" isn't just seeking and finding. Because, said the pope, "when he finds us, when he finds the lost sheep," he doesn't set it apart and quiz it: "Why did you get lost, why did you fall?" No, he brings it home. "We could say, if we force the meaning," he explained, that he "reintegrates, reintroduces" the person he has sought and found. So when the shepherd puts the lost sheep back among the other sheep, it's not told "you are lost" but "you are one of us." It has "every right," just as the coin found by the woman is "put back in the purse like the other coins. There's no difference between them." For "a God who seeks is a God who puts back all those he's found where they belong. And when he does this, he's a God who rejoices. God's joy isn't a sinner's death but life: it's a joy."

So the gospel parable shows "how far from God's heart were those people who murmured against Jesus. They didn't know him. They believed," said the pope, "that being religious, being good people," meant "always behaving well and politely, often just pretending to be polite. That's murmuring hypocrisy. Whereas God the Father's joy comes from love. He loves us." Even if we say, "but I'm a sinner: I've done, this and this and this…" God answers us: "I love you all the same and I go out and look for you and bring you home!" Thus, the pope concluded, "he's our Father."

THE TAINTED BREAD OF CORRUPTION

Friday, November 8, 2013
ROM 15:14-21; LK 16:1-8

Corrupt managers, "worshipers of the goddess of bribery," commit "a grave sin against dignity" and give "tainted bread" to their own children. We should counter this "worldly cunning" with "Christian cunning," which is "a gift of the Holy Spirit." That's what Pope Francis said in his homily at the Mass celebrated on Friday morning, November 8, in the chapel of St. Martha's House. He was reflecting on the figure of the unjust steward described in the liturgical passage from Luke's gospel (16:1-8).

"The Lord," said the pope, "speaks to us again about the spirit of the world, of worldliness: how this worldliness operates and how dangerous it is. In his prayer after the Last Supper, Jesus himself prayed to the Father that his disciples might not fall into worldliness," the spirit of the world.

Worldliness, the pope repeated, "is the enemy." And "the atmosphere, the lifestyle" typical of worldliness—that is, "living according to the world's 'values'"—is what "so delights the devil." So "when we think about our enemy, we should think first about the devil, because he's the one who does us harm."

"An example of worldliness" is the steward described in the gospel. "Any of you," observed the pope, "could say: but this man just did what everyone does." Actually, "not everyone!" This is the way "some managers, business managers, public managers, even some government managers behave. Perhaps not that many." Basically, "it's that attitude of taking a short cut, making it easier to earn a living." The gospel tells us that "the master praised this unjust steward." And that, commented the pope, "is praising bribery. The bribery mentality is a worldly habit that's very wrong." Certainly it's an attitude that has nothing to do with God.

In fact, he continued, "God has commanded us: take home bread earned by honest toil." Whereas "that steward, that manager, gave his children tainted bread. And his children, who perhaps went to expensive colleges, perhaps grew up in cultured surroundings, received filth as food from their father. For by bringing home tainted bread the father had lost his dignity. Perhaps, said the pope, "it begins with a small kickback, but it's like a drug." And even if the first kickback "is small, then comes another and another: and it ends in the illness of being addicted to bribery."

Here, he declared, we're facing "a very serious sin because it goes against dignity. That dignity which work gives us. We don't get it from bribery or from an addiction to worldly cunning. When we read someone writing in the paper or watch someone speaking on TV about corruption, perhaps we think corruption is just a word. Corruption means not earning your bread with dignity.

But there's another way, that of "Christian cunning"—"in quotes," said the pope—which allows us to "act smartly but not with the spirit of the world. Jesus himself said so: be cunning as serpents, innocent as doves." Putting "these two together" is "a grace" and "a gift of the Holy Spirit." So we must ask the Lord to enable us to be "honest in life, with that honesty which makes us work as we ought to work, without getting mixed up in those things." Pope Francis repeated: "This 'Christian cunning' —the serpent's cunning and the dove's innocence—is a gift, a gift the Lord gives us. But we have to ask for it."

Then Pope Francis' thoughts turned to the families of dishonest managers. "Perhaps today," he said, "it will do us all good to pray for so many children who get tainted bread from their parents. They too are hungry. They're hungry for dignity." Hence the invitation "to pray that the Lord will change the hearts of those who worship the goddess of bribery," so that they understand "that dignity comes from worthwhile work, honest work, everyday work, and not from those easy short cuts which end up taking everything away." For, he concluded, there's also the risk of ending up like the man in the gospel "who had so many barns, so many granaries, which were all full and he didn't know what to do about them. 'Tonight you must die,' said the Lord. Those poor people who have lost their dignity by practicing bribery can't take with them the money they've earned, only their loss of dignity. Let us pray for them."

WATER FLOWING THROUGH THE CHURCH

Saturday, November 9, 2013
Feast of the Dedication of the Lateran Basilica
EZEK 47:1-2, 8-9, 12; JN 2:13-22

We need to pray that the church may always allow the water of grace to flow, that she may always be founded upon Christ and remain faithful to him, and that her members may be converted to Christ every day. This is what Pope Francis recommended to the faithful who attended the Mass celebrated in St. Martha's chapel, this morning, Saturday, November 9.

The pope referred to the meaning of the liturgical feast of the dedication of the Lateran Basilica, the Rome cathedral whose title is "mother of all churches urbe et orbe." This he said, was the feast day of the city of Rome, the church of Rome, the universal church. Then he mentioned three images from the day's readings that are about the church. From the first reading (Ezekiel 47:1-2, 8-9, 12 and Psalm 46 (45), there was the image of the river of water gushing from the temple to gladden the city of God, an image of the grace that sustains and feeds the life of the church. From the second reading (1 Corinthians 3:9-11, 16-17) there was the image of the rock that is Christ, the foundation upon which the church is built. From the gospel of the cleansing of the temple (John 2:13-22), there was the image of the reform of the church: ecclesia semper reformanda. The church always needs to be renewed because her members are sinners and need to be converted.

SINNERS YES, CORRUPT NO

Monday, November 11, 2013
WIS 1:1-7; LK 17:1-6

"Sinners yes, corrupt no." During the Mass celebrated this morning, Monday, November 11, in St. Martha's chapel, Pope Francis spoke again about corruption, or rather about the corrupt people whose "double life" makes them like "a varnished rottenness."

The pope's reflection took its cue from a passage from Luke's gospel (17:1-6): "If your brother sins, you must rebuke the offender, and if he repents, you must forgive him. And if the same person sins against you seven times a day and turns back to you seven times a day and says: 'I repent,' you must forgive." In this, said the pope, "I always see a picture of Jesus. We've heard it so many times: he never tires of forgiving. And he advises us to do the same." The bishop of Rome then looked at the figure of the sinner who asks forgiveness, but even though he has really repented he falls again, and again, into sin. The pope explained, "He really repents but he can't stop sinning; he's weak. It's the weakness of original sin." There's the goodwill but also the weakness and "the Lord forgives." The only condition, added the pope, "is to go to him and say 'I've sinned, forgive me. I want to stop doing it but I'm weak.' That's the sinner." And Jesus' attitude is always to forgive.

In another part of the gospel passage, noted the bishop of Rome, Jesus says, "Woe to anyone by whom scandals come." Jesus, he explained, "isn't speaking about sin but about scandal," and he says: "It would be better for him if a millstone were hung around his neck and he was thrown into the sea, than for him to scandalize one of these little ones. Be on your guard!" So the pope asked: "But what's the difference between sin and scandal? What's the difference between committing a sin and doing something that causes scandal and does harm, so much harm?" The difference, he said, is that "the one who sins, repents and asks forgiveness, feels weak, feels he's a child of God, humiliates himself, and asks Jesus for salvation. But the one who causes scandal doesn't repent and goes on sinning and pretends to be a Christian." It's as if he were leading "a double life," and the pope added, "a Christian's double life does so much harm."

The pope gave the example of the person who puts his hand in his pocket and shows that he's giving help to the church, whereas with his other hand he's robbing "the state, the poor." That person "is the wrongdoer" for whom it would be better—

"and it's not me saying so but Jesus," stressed the pope—"that a millstone were hung round his neck and he was thrown into the sea." There's no question of forgiveness here "because that person is deceiving," said the pope. Then he referred to the first reading, taken from the book of Wisdom (1:1-7), where we read: "A holy and disciplined spirit will flee from deceit, and will leave foolish thoughts behind, and will be ashamed at the approach of unrighteousness."

"Where there's deceit," commented Pope Francis, "there isn't the Spirit of God. That's the difference between the sinner and the corrupt. The one who sins would like not to sin, but is weak or finds himself in a situation from which he can see no way out, but he goes to the Lord and asks for forgiveness. The Lord loves this person, stays with him. And we have to say, all of us who are here: sinners yes, corrupt no." But the corrupt, continued the pope, know nothing of humility. Jesus compared them to whitened sepulchers: beautiful on the outside but inside full of rotten bones. "And a Christian who boasts of being a Christian but doesn't lead a Christian life," he said, "is corrupt."

We all know someone who "is in this situation and we all know," he added, "how much harm these corrupt Christians, corrupt priests, do to the church. What a lot of harm they do the church! They don't live by the spirit of the gospel, but by the spirit of the world. And St. Paul tells the Romans clearly: 'Do not be conformed to this world' (cf. Romans 12:2). But in the original text it's even stronger: don't enter into the schemes of this world, the guidelines of this world, because it's these, this worldliness, that lead to a double life."

In conclusion the Holy Father said: "A varnished rottenness: that's what a corrupt person's life is like. And Jesus didn't call these people sinners. He called them hypocrites." Jesus, the pope reminded us, always forgives, never tires of forgiving. The only condition he asks for is that we don't want to lead that double life: "Let us ask the Lord today that we may shun all deceit, and recognize ourselves as sinners. Sinners yes, corrupt no."

In God's Safe Hands

Tuesday, November 12, 2013
Wis 2:23–3:9; Lk 17:7-10

In God's hands. That's where our safety lies. They are hands wounded by love that guide us on the way of life, not death, which is where envy leads us. This was the focus of Pope Francis' reflection this morning, Tuesday, November 12, during the Mass celebrated in St. Martha's chapel.

Introducing his homily, the Holy Father noted the first reading recalls that God "created human beings for incorruptibility" (Wisdom 2:23–3:9). He "made us and he's our Father. He made us beautiful like himself, more beautiful than the angels; greater than the angels. But, through the devil's envy, death came into the world."

Envy's a very clear word, the pope said, which enables us to understand the battle that took place between "this angel," the devil, and human beings. The former "couldn't endure the fact that human beings were superior to himself; that in man and woman there was the image and likeness of God. That's why he waged war" and introduced a way "that leads to death. That's how death came into the world."

Actually, continued the bishop of Rome "we all experience death." How can that be explained? "The Lord," he answered, "doesn't abandon his works," as the text from Wisdom says: "The just are in God's hands." We must all "undergo death. But it's one thing to experience it in the devil's hands and another to experience it in God's."

"I like hearing these words," he confided. "We're in God's hands. From the beginning. The Bible explains creation through a beautiful image: God makes us from mud, from clay, with his own hands, in his own image and likeness. God's hands created us: God the potter."

So he hasn't abandoned us. And we read in the Bible that he says to his people: "I have walked with you." God behaves like "a father who leads his child by the hand. God's own hands accompany us on the way." The Father teaches us to walk, to go "along the way of life and salvation." And again: "God's hands caress us in moments of pain, they comfort us. He's our Father caressing us, who loves us so much. And often in these caresses there's also forgiveness."

Something "that does me good," said the pope, "is thinking: Jesus, God, has carried his wounds with him. He shows them to the Father. That's the price: God's hands are hands wounded by love. And that's such a comfort to us. So often we've heard it said: I don't know where to turn, all the doors are shut, I'll put myself in God's hands! And that's lovely, because there we're safe," held in the hands of a Father who loves us.

God's hands, continued the Holy Father, "also heal us from our spiritual ills. Think of Jesus' hands when he touched the sick and healed them. They are God's hands. They heal us. I can't imagine a God who would hit us. I can't imagine it. Yes, I can imagine him rebuking us because he does so. But not him hurting us, never! He caresses us. Even when he has to rebuke us he does so with a caress, because he's a Father."

"The souls of the just are in God's hands," repeated the pope, concluding: "Let us think of God's hands, which created us like a potter. He gave us eternal salvation. They are wounded hands. They accompany us on life's way. Let us entrust ourselves into God's hands like children with their father." They are safe hands.

The Spirit of Wisdom Conquers Worldly Curiosity

Thursday, November 14, 2013
Wis 7:22b–8:1; Lk 17:20-25

At the Mass celebrated on Thursday morning, November 14, in St. Martha's House chapel, Pope Francis warned against the "spirit of worldly curiosity" and the desire to know the future that even tries to get hold of God's plans.

The pope took his cue from the first liturgical reading, taken from the book of Wisdom (7:22–8:1). He explained that the biblical passage "gives us a description of the state of mind of spiritual men and women," almost like a spiritual identity card of true Christians, who live "in the wisdom of the Holy Spirit." Wisdom founded on a "spirit that is intelligent, holy, unique, complex, subtle." The right attitude is to "carry on, say the saints, in a good spirit." So the Christian is called "to go through life in this spirit: the spirit of God, which helps us judge, make decisions according to God's heart. And this spirit always gives us peace. It's the spirit of peace, the spirit of love, the spirit of fellowship."

"Holiness," said the pope, "is that." It's "what God asks of Abraham: walk in my presence and be irreproachable. It's that, that peace." It's about "walking under the impulse of God's spirit and wisdom. And we can say that a man or woman who does that is a wise man or woman. They are wise men and women because they move with God's patience."

But, the pope continued, in the gospel passage from Luke (17:20-25) "we find another spirit that is contrary to the spirit of God's wisdom: the spirit of curiosity. It's when we want to get hold of God's projects, the future, to know everything, take everything in hand." In the passage from Luke we read that the Pharisees asked Jesus: "When will the kingdom of God come?"

And the pope commented: "They're curious! They want to know the date, the day ..."

It's this "spirit of curiosity," he explained, "that distances us from the spirit of wisdom," because it drives us to look only at "the details, the news, the little stories of the day: how will this happen? Wanting to know the 'how.'" According to the pope, "the spirit of curiosity isn't a good spirit. It's a scatter-brained spirit that distances us from God; it's the spirit of talking too much."

Jesus tells us "something interesting: this spirit of curiosity, which is worldly, leads to confusion." The Holy Father explained, referring to words in the gospel passage: "The days are coming when you will long to see one of the days of the Son of Man, and you will not see it. They will say to you, 'Look there!' or 'Look here!'" In that case, said the pope, "it's curiosity" that urges us "to hear such things. They tell us: The Lord is here, and there and here! But I know a visionary, a visionary who gets letters from the Madonna, messages from the Madonna." And the pope commented: "But look, the Madonna's not a postwoman who delivers messages every day." In fact, "these novelties distance us from the gospel, distance us from the Holy Spirit, from peace and wisdom, from God's glory, God's beauty."

So Pope Francis reiterated Jesus' teaching: the kingdom of God "doesn't arrive in a way that draws attention" but comes in wisdom; "the kingdom of God is in the midst of you." And "the kingdom of God is this work, this action of the Holy Spirit giving us wisdom, giving us peace. The kingdom of God doesn't come in confusion. Just as God didn't speak to Elijah in the wind, the storm, the typhoon. He spoke to him in the still small voice, the voice that was wisdom."

The pope suggested something that St. Therese of the Child Jesus had thought, a thought that was particularly dear to him. "Little St. Therese," he recalled, "said that she always had to restrain herself from the spirit of curiosity. When she was speaking to another nun who was telling a story about her family, or about some people, which was interrupted by something else, she always wanted to hear the end of the story. But she thought that wasn't God's spirit, because it's a scatter-brained spirit, a spirit of curiosity."

"The kingdom of God is in the midst of us," Pope Francis concluded, repeating the words of the gospel. And he invited us "not to seek for strange things, not to seek for novelties through worldly curiosity. Let us allow the spirit to carry us on with that wisdom that is a still small voice. That's the spirit of the kingdom of God which Jesus is talking about."

God's Weakness for the Prayer of His People

Saturday, November 16, 2013
Wis 18:14-16, 19:6-9; Lk 18:1-8

God has a weakness for the prayer of his people. So prayer is the true strength of human beings; we should never tire of knocking at the door of God's heart, and asking for help, because when he is called upon to defend his people, God is implacable.

Pope Francis reminded us of this during the Mass celebrated this morning, Saturday, November 16, at St. Martha's. Also present were the canons of the Vatican Basilica, cardinal archpriest of the Basilica of St. Peter's Angelo Comastri, and bishop delegate of the Fabric of St. Peter's Vittoria Lanzani.

Commenting on the readings for the day, the pope wanted first of all to stress the protection the Lord offers his children when they turn to him: "God grants, will grant, justice to his elect, when they cry to him day and night. He has done so before: when he called Moses and said to him, I have heard the cry and lament of my people. The Lord listens" (cf. Luke 18:1-8).

"In the first reading," said the pope, "we heard what the Lord did: that omnipotent word comes down like a mighty warrior. When the Lord takes up the defense of his people like that, he's a mighty warrior and he saves his people. He saves, he renews everything; everything created is refashioned, in its own nature as before." And he's like that, said the Holy Father, quoting again from the book of Wisdom (18:14-16; 19:6-9): "The Red Sea becomes an unhindered way and the raging waves become a grassy plain, where those protected by your hand passed through as one people, after gazing on marvelous wonders." The description of their salvation is poetic, the pope noted: "For they ranged like horses, and leapt like lambs, praising you, O Lord, who delivered them." "That's the power of the Lord," stressed the pope, "when he wants to save his people: he's strong. He's the Lord. Because he's heard his people's prayer; because he's felt in his heart that his elect were suffering."

But if that's God's strength, "what's human strength?" asked the pope. It was shown by the widow of whom the gospel speaks, he explained. She knocked continually at the judge's door. "Knocking," he repeated, "asking, complaining of many problems, many sufferings, and asking the Lord to free us from those sufferings, those sins, those problems." That is human strength, prayer, "even the humble person's prayer," because if God has a weakness, he explained, it's for his people's prayer. "It's God's weakness. The Lord is only weak about this."

The readings, said the bishop of Rome, give us food for thought about "God's power, which is so clear, so strong." The church speaks about it especially at Christmas time, because "the culmination of God's power, God's salvation, was the incarnation of the Word: 'For while deep silence enveloped all things, and night in its swift course was now half gone, your all-powerful word leapt from heaven, from the royal throne, into the midst of the land that was doomed, a mighty warrior, carrying the sharp sword of your authentic command.' The church takes this text about liberation and strength to mean that the incarnation of the Word was the high point of our salvation."

"I like hearing these readings today with you canons of St. Peter's present," confided the pope. "Your work is indeed to knock at the door of God's heart," to pray. "Pray to the Lord for God's people. And you at St. Peter's, the basilica closest to the pope, where all the petitions in the world converge, you gather up these petitions and present them to the Lord with your prayers."

And to reinforce the idea of the service they are called upon to give, the pope returned to the tenacity of the widow in the gospel, who kept on and on at the judge, asking for justice. "Yours is a universal service, a service for the church. You're like the widow: praying, asking, knocking at the door of God's heart. Every day. And while she was doing this the widow never slept. She was brave."

"The Lord listens to his people's prayer," continued the Holy Father. "You are privileged representatives of God's people in this praying to the Lord for the many needs of the church, humanity, everyone." And in conclusion he said: "I thank you for this work. Let us always remember that God has a strength—when he wants—that changes everything. He is able to refashion everything. But he also has a weakness for our prayer, our universal prayer, close to the pope in St. Peter's. Thank you for this your service and keep it going for the good of the church."

Faithfulness to God Isn't Negotiable

Monday, November 18, 2013
1 Macc 1:10-15, 41-43, 54-57, 62-63; Lk 18:35-43

There's a hidden danger running through the world. It's the danger of globalization of hegemonic uniformity. It's characterized by a "single way of thinking," by which in the name of "adolescent progressivism" people don' hesitate to deny their own traditions and identity. However, we can be comforted by the fact that we always have the Lord with us, who is faithful to his promise. He awaits, loves us, protects us. In his hands we can walk safely along any road. This was Pope Francis' reflection on Monday morning, November 18, during the Mass at St. Martha's. Secretary of State Archbishop Pietro Parolin, who began his service at the Vatican today, concelebrated with the pope.

The pope began his reflection by commenting on the reading taken from the first book of Maccabees (1:10-15, 41-43, 54-57, 62-64). This was "one of the saddest pages in the Bible," he said. It speaks of "a good many of God's people deciding to move away from the Lord toward worldliness." This, noted the pope, was a typical example of that "spiritual worldliness that Jesus didn't want for us. He even prayed the Father to save us from the spirit of the world."

That worldliness has a perverse root. It comes from "evil people who are capable of clever persuasion: 'Let's go and make an alliance with the nations round us. We can't remain isolated,' sticking to our own traditions. 'Let's make an alliance, for since we have been separate from them, many bad things have happened to us.'" That way of reasoning, recalled the pope, was considered right, so some "took the initiative and went to the king, to make a deal with the king, negotiate." These people, he added, "were enthusiastic, they believed that in this way the nation, the people of Israel, would become a great nation." Of course, the pope noted, they did not ask themselves whether it was right or not to assume that progressivist attitude, which they understood as advancing at all costs. So they said: "We won't become shut off. We're progressive." It's a bit like what happens today, noted the bishop of Rome. It is "the spirit of adolescent progressivism," according to which, when faced with any choice, people think it's right to advance rather than remaining faithful to their own traditions. "These people," continued he pope, returning to the biblical story, "made a deal with the king, they negotiated. But they didn't negotiate habits… They negotiated their faithfulness to God, who is always faithful. And that's called apostasy. When they talked about unfaithfulness, the prophets called it adultery, an adulterous people. Jesus says so: "'adulterous and wicked generation,' who negotiate away something essential to their very being, their faithfulness to the Lord." Perhaps they don't negotiate some values, which they don't renounce. But these values, noted the pope, end up being so emptied of meaning that they become "nominal, unreal values."

All this has consequences, a price to be paid. Referring to the biblical story, the pope recalled that they adopted "pagan habits" and accepted the orders of the king, who "decreed that in his kingdom all would be one single people and that all should abandon their own particular customs." This, said the pope, certainly wasn't "beautiful globalization," which is expressed in "the unity of all nations," who nevertheless keep their own customs. What the story is talking about is "the globalization of hegemonic uniformity." It's "a single way of thinking caused by worldliness."

After reminding us of the consequences for those of the people of Israel who accepted this "single way of thinking" and engaged in sacrilegious acts, Pope Francis stressed that similar behavior can be found today: "today too the spirit of worldliness leads us to this desire to be progressive, to complicity with that single way of thinking." So just as happened then, when anyone found in possession of the book of the covenant was condemned to death, it happens today in different parts of the world "as we've read in the newspapers in recent months."

Negotiating away our own faithfulness to God is like negotiating away our identity. And here the pope recalled the book

Lord of the World by Robert Hugh Benson, son of the archbishop of Canterbury Edward White Benson. In this book the author speaks of the spirit of the world "and almost as if it were a prophecy, he imagines what will happen. This man, Benson, later converted to Catholicism and did a lot of good. He'd seen that spirit of worldliness which leads to apostasy." It will also do us good, suggested the pope, to think about what is written in the book of Maccabees, to what happened there, step by step, if we decide to follow this "adolescent progressivism" and do what everyone else does. And it will also do us good to think about what happened later in the story, when it led to "condemnations to death and human sacrifices." And when he asked: "Do you think there are no human sacrifices today?" he replied: "There are so many, so many. And there are laws that protect them."

But what can comfort us, the pope concluded, is that "besides the way pointed to by the spirit of the world, the prince of this world," the way of unfaithfulness, the Lord always remains and he can't deny himself; he is faithful. He always waits for us; he loves us so much, and is ready to forgive us, even if we take a little step along the way of the world. He always takes us by the hand, as he did with his beloved people, to lead us out of the desert.

Granddad's Table

Tuesday, November 19, 2013
2 Macc 6:18-31; Lk 19:1-10

Pope Francis again praised the important part played by old people in the church and society. He spoke about it during the Mass celebrated this morning, Tuesday, November 19, in St. Martha's chapel.

He began his homily with a question: "What legacy are we leaving our young people?" To answer it, the pope referred to the story in the second book of Maccabees (6:18-31), which tells about the wise old man Eleazar, a highly respected scribe, who rather than eat forbidden meat to please the king, voluntarily suffered martyrdom. He wouldn't listen to his friends' advice that he should pretend to eat the food in order to save himself. He preferred to die a painful death rather than give a bad example to others, especially the young. "An old man who was consistent to the end," said the Holy Father, in whose exemplary behavior we can see "the role of old people in the church and the world." "This man," he explained, "didn't not hesitate when the choice was between apostasy and faithfulness. He had so many friends. They wanted him to compromise: 'Pretend. That way you can stay alive...'" It's that attitude of pretense, pretending to be pious, pretending to be religious, that Jesus condemns with a very harsh word in Chapter 23 of Matthew's gospel: hypocrisy. Whereas "this good ninety-year-old, an honest old man much respected by his people, didn't think of himself. He only thought of God, how not to offend him by the sin of hypocrisy and apostasy. But he also thought about the legacy" he would leave. So he thought about the young. And in the biblical text, noted Pope Francis, even though it's talking about an old man, the word young often occurs. And he asked: "Which have I tried to follow all my life: a half-and-half compromise, hypocrisy or truth?" But we have here "the consistency of this man, the consistency of his faith," commented the bishop of Rome, "and also his sense of the responsibility to leave behind a true, noble legacy."

"We're living at a time when old people don't count. Sad to say," repeated the Holy Father, "they are rejected because they're a nuisance." Yet "old people are the ones who bring us history, doctrine, faith and leave it to us as a legacy. They are like good old wine, they have within them the power to give us that noble legacy."

Then the Pope referred to the witness of another grand old man, Polycarp. Condemned to be burned at the stake, "when the fire started to burn him," the pope recalled, there was a smell of newly baked bread. Such are old people. "Legacy, good wine and good bread." But "especially in our world they are considered a nuisance."

Here the pope returned to a memory of his childhood. "I remember," he said, "that when we were children we were told this story. There was a family, a father, a mother, and lots of children. There was also a grandfather living with them. But he was old and when he was at table eating soup he was very messy: he got soup on his mouth, his napkin... he looked a sight! One day the father told him that, as this was happening, from now on he'd have to eat alone. And he bought a little table and put it in the kitchen. So the grandfather ate alone in the kitchen and the family in the dining room. A few days later the father came home and saw one of his children playing with wood. He asked him: 'What are you doing?' 'I'm playing at being a carpenter,' the child replied. 'What are you making?' 'A little table for you, Daddy, for when you get old like Granddad.' That story did me so much good all my life. Grandparents are a treasure."

Returning to the scriptural teaching about old people, Pope Francis referred to the letter to the Hebrews (13:7), "in which we read: 'Remember your leaders, those who spoke the word of God to you; consider the outcome of their way of life, and imitate their faith.' Remembering our predecessors leads us to imitating their faith. It's true, sometimes old age is rather ugly because of the illnesses that go with it. But the wisdom our grandparents have is their legacy to us. A country that doesn't look after its grandparents, that doesn't respect its grandparents, has no future because it's lost its memory. Facing martyrdom, Eleazar is aware of his responsibility to the young. He thinks of God but he also thinks of the young: 'I must give the young an example of being consistent to the end.'"

"It will do us good to think of so many old men and women, all those who are in care homes and all those who—sad to say—have been abandoned by their families," added the Holy Father, reminding us that "these are our society's treasure. Let us pray for them to remain consistent to the end. That's the role of old people, that's the treasure. Let us pray for our grandfathers and grandmothers, who have so often played a heroic part in handing on the faith in times of persecution." And especially in times gone by when the children's fathers and mothers often weren't at home or had strange, confused ideas from the ideologies in fashion at the time, "it was actually the grandmothers who handed on the faith."

Why We Go to the Temple

Friday, November 22, 2013
1 Macc 4:36-37, 52-59; Lk 19:45-48

The temple exists "to worship God." That's why it's "the community's reference point," composed of people who are themselves "a spiritual temple where the Holy Spirit dwells." Pope Francis offered a meditation on "the true meaning of the temple" in his homily at the Mass celebrated this morning, Friday, November 22, in the chapel of St. Martha's House.

As usual the pope's reflection was based on the passages from the liturgy of the word, in particular the passage from the first book of Maccabees (4:36-37, 52-59)—about the re-dedication of the temple by Judas Maccabeus—and the gospel passage from Luke which tells of Jesus' cleansing of the temple (19:45-48).

The temple rededication by Judas Maccabeus, he explained,

was not the first time the temple had been rededicated and cleansed. In the vicissitudes of history the temple had been "destroyed" in wars and we "remember when Nehemiah rebuilt the temple." And so after his victory Judas Maccabeus thinks of the temple: "See, our enemies are crushed; let us go up to cleanse the sanctuary and dedicate it." The cleansing and rededication were necessary, "because the pagans had used the sanctuary for their own cult." So "it had to be cleansed and rededicated."

For Pope Francis the basic message "is so important: the temple is the community's reference point, the reference point of the people of God." And here the pope recalled "the temple's course through history," which "begins with the ark; then Solomon builds the temple; then it becomes a living temple: Jesus Christ. And it will end in glory, in the heavenly Jerusalem."

"Rededicating the temple so that glory can be given there to God" is the essential meaning of Judas Maccabeus' action, because "the temple is the place where the community goes to pray, to praise the Lord, to give thanks, but above all to worship." Indeed, "the Lord is worshiped in the temple. That's the most important point," the pope insisted. And that goes for every temple and every liturgical ceremony, where "what's most important is worship" and not "the songs and rituals," however beautiful. "The whole community together, he explained, looks towards the altar, where the sacrifice is being offered, and worships. But I believe—I say this humbly—that perhaps we Christians have rather lost the sense of worship. And we think: let's go to the temple, we'll meet together as brothers and sisters; and that's good, that's fine. But the heart is there where God is. And we worship God."

So Pope Francis invited us to take the opportunity to think again about the attitude we should have: "Are our temples places for worship?" he asked. "Do they encourage worship? Do our celebrations encourage worship?" Judas Maccabeus and the people "were filled with zeal for God's temple because it's God's house, God's home. And they went as a community to seek God there, to worship."

As Luke the evangelist tells us, "Jesus also cleanses the temple." But he does so "with whip in hand." He drives out "pagan ways, in this case the behavior of the traders who were buying and selling and had turned the temple into little shops to buy and sell money, for money and currency exchange." Jesus cleanses the temple declaring: "It's written: my house shall be a house of prayer" and "not anything else. The temple is a holy place. And we should enter into its holiness to worship. Not for anything else."

Besides, continued the pope, "St. Paul tells us that we are temples of the Holy Spirit: I am a temple, the spirit of God is in me. And he also tells us: do not grieve the spirit of the Lord that is in you." So, the pope said, we can speak of "a kind of worship which is the heart seeking the spirit of the Lord within itself. And the heart knows that God is within it, the Holy Spirit is within it. The heart listens and follows that Spirit. And we too," he declared, "must constantly cleanse ourselves because we're sinners: cleanse ourselves by prayer, by penance, by the sacrament of reconciliation, by the Eucharist."

And thus, explained the Holy Father, "in these two temples— the material temple, which is a place of worship, and the spiritual temple within me where the Holy Spirit dwells—our attitude should be a devotion that worships and listens; that prays and asks for forgiveness; that praises the Lord." And "when the joy of the temple is spoken of, that's what it means: the whole community worshiping, praying, giving thanks, praising. And also myself as a temple: me in prayer with the Lord who is within me; me listening; me in readiness."

Pope Francis ended his homily by inviting us to pray that "the Lord may grant us a true sense of the temple, so that we may go forward in our life of worship and listening to God's word."

Courage to Make Hard Choices

Monday, November 25, 2013
Dan 1:1-6, 8-20; Lk 21:1-4

How often do Christians—those who are "being persecuted today" or even "mothers and fathers of families—find themselves in "extreme situations?" And when they are forced to make hard choices do they choose the Lord? Pope Francis asked this in his homily at the Mass celebrated on Monday morning, November 25, at St. Martha's. He stressed that these choices are very difficult, so we must ask the Lord "for the grace of courage."

The pope began by referring to the liturgical passage taken from the book of the prophet Daniel (1:1-6, 8-20), which tells the story of some young men who found the courage to refuse the contaminated food ordered by the king and managed to feed themselves secretly on just water and vegetables. The Lord repays their faithfulness by helping them to develop a more agile body and mind than all the others, so that they became the king's favorites. Those young men, noted the Holy Father, were "on the edge because they were slaves, and when at that time—but also today—you fell into slavery nothing was safe anymore, not even your life. We're on the edge."

The bishop of Rome then recalled the episode in Luke's gospel (21:1-4) of the widow's coin. She hasn't even got anything to eat herself but nevertheless she offers all she has. "Jesus tells us," stressed the pope, "that she was very poor. At that time widows didn't have their husband's pension; they lived in poverty. They were on the edge." So those young men and that widow were on the edge when they found they had to make a decision.

"The widow," noted the pope, "went to the temple to worship God, to tell the Lord that he's above everything and that she loves him." She feels she has to do something for the Lord and "gives all that she has to live on." And this action of hers "is something more than generosity, it's something else." She chooses well: the Lord alone. Because "she forgets herself. She could have said: but Lord, you know, I need this money for food today ... and put the money back in her pocket. Instead she chose to worship the Lord to the end."

The young men also had the chance to find "an emergency way out, we could call it, from their situation," added the bishop of Rome. They could have said: "But we're slaves. The law can't be kept here; we must save our lives, not get thin or ill... Let's eat!" Instead, "they said no. They made a good choice: the Lord." They were intelligent enough to find a way of remaining faithful, even in that difficult situation.

The young men and the widow, said the Holy Father, "took a risk. They risked choosing the Lord." They did so with their hearts. They didn't do it for personal gain or from narrow-mindedness. They entrusted themselves to the Lord. And they didn't do it, noted Pope Francis, out of fanaticism, "but because they knew that the Lord is faithful. They entrusted themselves to that faithfulness which never fails." Because "the Lord is always faithful" in that "he can't deny himself."

Entrusting ourselves to the Lord's faithfulness is a choice, said the pope, "which we also have the opportunity to make in our Christian lives." Sometimes this means making "a big, difficult choice." In the history of the church, even in our own time, there are men and women, old and young, who make that choice. We realize this "when we know about the lives of martyrs, when we read in the newspapers about the persecution of Christians today. Let us think of those brothers and sisters who are in these extreme situations and who make that choice. They are living in our own time. They are an example for us. They encourage us to throw into the church's treasury everything we have to live on."

Returning to the young men in the book of the prophet Daniel, the Holy Father noted that the Lord "helps them and gets them out of difficulty; they are victorious and it ends well for them." The Lord also helps the widow in Luke's gospel, "because behind Jesus' praise of her, God is praising her: truly I tell you this widow... It's a victory. It will do us good to think of those brothers and sisters, who, throughout history and today, have made definitive choices." The pope invited us to think in particular of "so many mothers and fathers of families who make hard choices every day to look after their family, to keep things going with their children. And that's a treasure in the church." With so many who continue today to bear witness, to show us, he concluded, "let us ask for the grace of courage. Courage to go forward in our Christian life, in everyday things and in extreme situations."

The Master of Time

Tuesday, November 26, 2013
Dan 2:31-45; Lk 21:5-11

Woe betide us if we delude ourselves that we are masters of our time. We can be masters of the moment we're living in, but time belongs to God and he gives us the hope to live through it. There is so much confusion today about who time actually belongs to but we shouldn't deceive ourselves. This is what Pope Francis said in his homily at the Mass celebrated on Tuesday morning, November 26, in St. Martha's chapel. And he explained why and how, reflecting on what is said in the readings of this final period of the liturgical year, during which "the church makes us think about the end."

St. Paul, noted the pope, "so often returns to this and puts it very clearly: 'The form of this world will disappear.' But that's something else. The readings often speak about destruction, ending, disaster." We must all take the road that leads to the end, each one of us, all humanity. But while we walk along it, "the Lord advises us to do two things," said the pope, "two things that are different according to how we live. For one thing, to live in the moment, and another, to live in time." And he stressed: "The Christian is the man or woman who knows how to live in the moment and how to live in time."

The moment, added the bishop of Rome, is what we have to hand in the instant we're living in. But it shouldn't be confused with time, because the moment passes. "Perhaps," he pointed out, "we can feel we're masters of the moment. But," he added, "the mistake is to think we're masers of time. Time doesn't belong to us. It belongs to God." Of course, the moment is in our hands and we're free to take it as we like best, the pope explained. So "we can become lords of the moment. But there's only one lord of time: Jesus Christ. So the Lord advises us: 'Beware that you are not led astray: for many will come in my name and say: "I am he!" and "The time is near!" Do not go after them' (Luke 21:8; cf. Mark 13:6). Don't let yourselves be led astray into confusion."

But how is it possible to defeat these delusions? The Christian, explained the Holy Father, must be guided by prayer and discernment in order to live in the moment without being led astray. "Jesus rebukes those who can't discern the moment," added the pope and went on to refer to the parable of the fig tree (Mark 13:28-29), in which Christ reprimands those who can tell that summer is coming, because the fig tree is sprouting, but can't recognize the signs of "this moment, as part of God's time."

That's what discernment is for, he explained, "to recognize the true signs, to know the way we must go at this moment." Prayer, continued the pope, is necessary to live this moment well.

But as regards time, "over which only the Lord is master," repeated the pope, we can do nothing. In fact there's no human quality that can enable us to have power over time. The only possible quality to deal with time "has to be given by the Lord: it's hope."

Prayer and discernment for the moment; hope for time: "that's how the Christian lives each moment, with prayer and discernment. But for time there's hope. The Christian knows how to await the Lord at any moment, but hopes in the Lord at the end of time. Men and women of the moment and of time, of prayer and discernment and of hope."

And the pope's final prayer was: "May the Lord give us the grace to walk with wisdom. That's also a gift: the wisdom that leads us to prayer and discernment for the moment and for time, which is God's messenger, it makes us live in hope."

FAITH IS NEVER A PRIVATE MATTER

Thursday, November 28, 2013
DAN 6:12-28; LK 21:20-28

The prohibition against worshiping God is a sign of "general apostasy," and it's the great temptation that tries to convince Christians to go "a more reasonable, peaceful way," obeying "the orders of worldly powers" who claim to consign "religion to a private matter." And above all they don't want God to be worshiped "with trust and faithfulness." Pope Francis warned against that very temptation at the Mass celebrated on Thursday, November 28, in St. Martha's chapel.

As usual the pope took his cue from the liturgy of the word, which, he stressed, "makes us think about the last days, the end time, the end of the world, the time of the final coming of our Lord Jesus Christ." In fact, he explained, "each of us has temptations in our lives. So many temptations. The devil presses us not to be faithful to the Lord. Sometimes he presses us hard." Like that time Jesus spoke about to Peter: "the devil wanted to sift him like wheat. We've so often been tempted and, since we're sinners, we've fallen." But the liturgy today, said the pope, "speaks of the universal temptation, the universal test, the moment when all creation, all the Lord's creation, will be put to the test to choose between God and evil, between God and the prince of this world."

Besides, he continued, "the devil started putting Jesus to the test at the beginning of his life, in the wilderness. And the devil tried to persuade him to go a different, more reasonable, more peaceful way that was less dangerous. In the end he made plain his intention: if you worship me I'll give you this! He wanted to be Jesus' God." And then Jesus himself, declared the pope, had "so many tests in his public life: insults, slanders," or when people approached him hypocritically "to put him to the test." And also "at the end of his life he was put to the test by the prince of this world on the cross: 'But if you are the Son of God come down and we'll all believe in you!'" But in the end Jesus rose from the dead "according to the Father's will, not that of the devil."

In today's liturgy, said the pope "the church makes us think about the end of this world, because it will come to an end. The form of this world will disappear." And there's a word in the gospel "that is very striking: all these things will come." But how long must we wait? The answer Luke's gospel (Luke 21:20-28) gives us is "until the times of the Gentiles are fulfilled." For, said the pope, "the Gentiles also have a time of fulfillment: the kairos of the Gentiles. They have a kairos, a time, he repeated, which will be their ultimate final triumph: the destruction of Jerusalem." And we read in the gospel, "there will be signs in the sun, the moon and the stars, and on the earth distress among nations confused by the roaring of the sea and the waves. People will faint from fear and foreboding of what is coming upon the world. Then the powers of heaven will be shaken."

Actually, "it's disaster," said the pope. "But when Jesus speaks about this disaster in another passage, he says there will a profanation of the temple, a profanation of the faith, and of the people. It will be the abomination. It will be the abomination of desolation (Daniel 9:27). What does that mean? It will be like the triumph of the prince of this world, the defeat of God. It appears that at this final moment of disaster, the devil will take power over this world," so he will become "master of the world."

Then Pope Francis explained how "this battle between the living God and the prince of this world" can be found in the first reading, taken from the book of the prophet Daniel (6:12-28). "Daniel is condemned just for worshiping, worshiping God. And the abomination of desolation is called prohibition to worship."

At that time, explained the pope, "you couldn't speak about religion: it was a private matter." Religious symbols were removed and you had to obey the orders coming from "the worldly powers." You could "do so many things, fine things, but you couldn't worship God," it was forbidden. This was "that pagan attitude's time." But just when "that time is fulfilled, then he will come." As we read in the gospel passage: "They will see the Son of Man coming in a cloud with power and great glory."

God's word tells us, continued the pope, how "Christians who suffer times of persecution, times when worship is forbidden, are a prophecy of what will happen to us all." But at those very moments, when the times of the pagans are fulfilled: "Stand up and raise your heads because your redemption is drawing near." In fact, explained the bishop of Rome, "the triumph, the victory of Jesus Christ, is to bring creation to the Father at the end of time."

But we mustn't be afraid. The pope repeated God's promise, which "asks us for faithfulness and patience. Faithfulness like Daniel's, who was faithful to his God and worshiped God to the end. And patience, because the hairs of our heads won't fall, the Lord has promised us." And the pope concluded by inviting us to reflect, especially this week, on "that general apostasy which is called the prohibition to worship." And we should ask ourselves: "'Do I worship the Lord? Do I worship Jesus Christ the Lord? Or do I half worship and then flirt with the prince of this world?' We should ask for the grace to worship to the end with trust and faithfulness."

FREE THOUGHT

Friday, November 29, 2013
DAN 7:2-14; LK 21:29-33

During the Mass celebrated at St. Martha's this morning, Friday, November 29, Pope Francis invited us "to think as Christians," since "Christians don't only think with their heads but also with heart and spirit." He said this invitation is especially urgent in a social context where there is ever more pressure from "weak thinking, a single way of thinking, a readymade way of thinking."

The bishop of Rome focused his reflection on the gospel passage from Luke (21:29-33) in the day's liturgy, in which the Lord "teaches the disciples by simple examples to understand what is happening." In this case Jesus invites them to look at "the fig tree and all the trees," because when they sprout we know that summer is coming. In other contexts the Lord uses analogous examples to rebuke the Pharisees, who don't want to understand "the signs of the times"; those who don't see "God's passage through history," through the history of the people of Israel, the history of the human heart, "the history of humanity."

According to the Holy Father, the teaching is that "Jesus encourages us in simple words to think and understand." It's an encouragement to think "not only with our heads," but also "with heart and spirit," with our whole selves. And that is precisely what "thinking as Christians" means, so that we can "understand the signs of the times." And Christ calls those who don't understand, like the disciples on the road to Emmaus, "foolish and slow of heart." Because, the pope explained, those who "don't understand the things of God are like that," foolish and slow to understand, whereas "the Lord wants us to understand what's happening in our hearts, our lives, the world, in history." He wants us to understand "the meaning of what's happening now." In fact, it's by answering these questions that we can discern "the signs of the times."

However, things don't always go like that. There's an enemy lying in wait. It's "the spirit of the world," which, said the Holy Father, "has other ideas for us." Because "it doesn't want a people, it wants 'the masses.' Thoughtless and unfree. Essentially, the spirit of the world drives us along "a way of uniformity, but without that spirit that embodies a people." It treats us "as if we had no power to think, as unfree." And Pope Francis expressly clarified the mechanisms of hidden persuasion: there's a particular way of thinking that must be imposed; "there's publicity for this way of thinking" and "we have to think" in that way. It's "a single way of thinking, the same way of thinking, a feeble way of thinking," but a way of thinking that is "so widespread," said the bishop of Rome.

In practice "the spirit of the world doesn't want us to ask God: but why is this happening?" And to distract us from these vital questions "it offers us a readymade way of thinking, according to our wishes: I'll think as I please." That way of thinking "is fine" for the spirit of the world. But the spirit of the world "doesn't want what Jesus asks of us: free thinking, the thinking of a man or woman belonging to the people of God." For "that's what salvation is: making us a people, the people of God. With freedom." Because "Jesus asks us to think freely, to think in order to understand what's happening."

Of course, warned Pope Francis, "we can't do it all alone: we need help from the Lord, we need the Holy Spirit to understand the signs of the times." In fact it's the Spirit who gives us "the intelligence to understand." It's a personal gift given to each of us, thanks to which "I have to understand why this is happening to me" and "what way the Lord wants me to go" in my life. This led to the pope's final exhortation, to "ask the Lord Jesus for the grace to send us his spirit of intelligence," so that "we don't go for feeble thinking, uniform thinking, thinking according to our wishes," but that we may "only think in accordance with God." And "with that way of thinking—with mind, heart, and spirit—which is a gift of the Spirit," may we try to understand "what things mean, understand well the signs of the times."

MEETING JESUS WITH OUR DEFENSES DOWN

Monday, December 2, 2013
ISA 4:2-6; MT 8:5-11

Let us meet Jesus "with our defenses down, openly," so that he can renew us in the depths of our soul. That was Pope Francis' invitation at the beginning of the season of Advent, which he offered the faithful during the Mass celebrated his morning, Monday, December 2, in St. Martha's chapel.

The road we set out on in the coming days, he said, is "a new journey for the church, a journey of the people of God toward Christmas. We're going to meet the Lord." For Christmas is a meeting, not just "a recurring event" or, said the pope, just "a memory of something beautiful. Christmas is more than that. We follow this road to meet the Lord." So during the season of Advent, "let us go to meet him. Meet him in our hearts, our lives; meet him as someone alive; meet him with faith."

Really, it isn't "easy to live by faith," noted the bishop of Rome. And he recalled the episode of the centurion who, according to the account in Matthew's gospel (8:5-11), falls down before Jesus to ask him to heal his slave. "In the passage we've just heard," explained the pope, "the Lord marvels at this centurion. He marveled at the faith he had. He'd made a journey to meet the Lord. He'd made it in faith. So he not only met the Lord but felt the joy of being met by the Lord. And that's just the meeting we want, the meeting of faith. Meeting the Lord, but also letting ourselves be met by him. That's very important!"

When we limit ourselves to just meeting the Lord, he explained, "we're the 'masters'—in inverted commas—of that meeting." But when "we let ourselves be met by him, he's the one who comes to us, into us" and renews us completely. That, repeated the Holy Father, "is what it means for Christ to come: remaking everything, remaking heart, soul, life, hope, the way to go."

So, in this season of the liturgical year, we're on the way to meet the Lord, but also and above all, to "letting ourselves be met by him." And we must do so with an open heart, "so that he meets me, tells me what he wants to say to me, which isn't always what I want him to say to me!" So let's not forget that "he's the Lord and he'll tell me what he wants for me," for each of us, because "the Lord," said the pope, "doesn't look at us all together in a mass: no, no! He looks at each of us one by one, in the face, in the eyes, because his love isn't abstract but very particular. Person to person. The Lord, a person, looks at me, a person." That's why letting ourselves be met by the Lord means finally "letting ourselves be loved by the Lord."

"In the prayer at the beginning of the Mass," recalled the pope, "we asked for the grace to go this way with some attitudes that will help us. Perseverance in prayer: praying more. Active kindness: coming a bit closer to those in need. And joy in praising the Lord." So "let us begin with prayer, kindness and praise, with an open heart, so that the Lord may meet us." But, the pope begged in "conclusion, please may we meet him openly, with our defenses down!"

Peace That Is Loud with Praise

Tuesday, December 3, 2013
Isa 11:1-10; Lk 10:21-24

We can't think of the church without joy, because Jesus, her bridegroom, was full of joy. So all Christians should live with that same joy in their hearts and pass it on to the ends of the earth. That, in brief, was what Pope Francis said in his reflection this morning, Tuesday, December 3, in his homily during the Mass celebrated in St. Martha's chapel in memory of the great preacher of the gospel, Francesco Saverio.

"God's word today," the pope began, "speaks to us of peace and joy. In his prophecy Isaiah (11:1-10) tells us what the days of the Messiah will be like. They will be days of peace." For, he explained, Jesus will bring peace between us and God, and peace between each other. So the peace we all long for is that brought by the Messiah.

Luke's gospel (10:21-24), read in today's liturgy, helps us understand something else about Jesus. "We get a glimpse into

Jesus' soul, Jesus' heart. It's a joyful heart." We're used to thinking of Jesus preaching, healing, going about talking to people, or
when he's on the cross. But "we're not so accustomed," said the
bishop of Rome, "to thinking of Jesus smiling, cheerful. Jesus
was full of joy." A joy that came from his closeness to the Father.
It's that relationship with his Father in the Spirit that gives rise
to Jesus' inner joy. Joy, the Holy Father added, which "he gives
to us. And that joy is true peace. It's not a static, calm, tranquil
peace: Christian peace is a joyful peace," because Jesus is joyful,
God is joyful.

"In the prayer at the beginning of Mass," he continued, "we
asked for the grace of missionary fervor, so that the church may
be gladdened by new children." We can't think of "a church without joy," because "Jesus wanted the church, his bride, to be joyful."
And "the church's joy is to proclaim the name of Jesus," to be able
to say, "My bridegroom is the Lord, is God" who "saves us" and
"is with us."

In her bridal joy the church "becomes a mother. Paul VI," said
Pope Francis recalling the teaching of his predecessor, "said the
church's joy is to preach the gospel" and pass on that joy "to her
children." So we understand that the peace that "Isaiah speaks
to us about," he continued, "is a joyful peace, a praiseful peace, a
peace, we could say, that is loud with praise. A peace that bears
fruit in mothering new children, a peace that comes from the joy
of praising the Trinity and preaching the gospel, that is, going out
to tell people who Jesus is."

So, peace and joy. "Always joy, because," the Holy Father explained, "it comes from what Jesus said: you decided not to reveal
yourself to the wise but to little ones. Even in things as serious
as this, Jesus is joyful." So the church must be joyful too. Always,
even "during her grass widowhood," he added, she "is joyful in
hope." "Let us pray," he concluded, "that the Lord may give this
joy to all of us."

WILD WORDS

Thursday, December 5, 2013
ISA 26:1-6; MT 7:21, 24-27

"Christian words" that are empty of Christ's presence are like wild words that make no sense and are deceitful. Pope Francis invited us to make "an examination of conscience" on whether what we say and what we do are consistent, during the Mass celebrated on Thursday morning, December 5, in the chapel of St. Martha's House.

Taking his cue from the liturgy for the day, the pope recalled that "the Lord often spoke of this attitude," knowing the word without putting it into practice. As the gospel tells us, Jesus "also rebuked the Pharisees," for "knowing everything, but not doing it." And so "he told people: do what they tell you but not what they do, because they don't do what they say!" It's a matter of either "words without deeds" or words that are put into practice. However, those "are good words," said the pope, "they are beautiful words." For example, "the commandments and the Beatitudes" are among those "good words," as well as "so many things that Jesus said. We can repeat them, but if we don't carry them out in our lives, not only are they of no use, but they do harm, they deceive us, they make us think we have a fine house, but it has no foundation."

In the gospel passage from Matthew (7:21-27), the pope continued, the Lord tells us that anyone "who hears the word and puts it into practice will be like a wise man who builds his house upon a rock." It comes down to a "mathematical equation: I know the word—I put it into practice—I'm built on a rock." But the essential point, said the Holy Father, is "how do I put it into practice?" And the point of Jesus' message is to put it into practice like building a house on a rock." And "the image of the rock refers to the Lord."

Pope Francis then turned to the prophet Isaiah, who said in the first reading (26:1-6), "Trust in the Lord forever, for in the Lord you have an everlasting rock." So, the pope explained, "the rock is Jesus Christ, the rock is the Lord. A word is strong, life-giving; it can go forward, withstand all the attacks, if that word is rooted in Jesus Christ." On the other hand, "a Christian word that doesn't have its vital roots in the life of a person, in Jesus Christ, is a Christian word without Christ. And Christian words without Christ deceive us; they do us harm."

Then the pope recalled the English writer G.K. Chesterton (1874–1936), who "when he spoke about heresies" said "a heresy is a truth, a word, a truth that has gone mad." It is a fact, stressed the pope, that "when Christian words are without Christ they begin to go the way madness lies." Isaiah, he continued, "is clear and he tells us what this madness is." In the biblical passage we read: "The Lord is an everlasting rock because he has brought low the inhabitants of the height; the lofty city he lays low." Yes, "the inhabitants of the height. A Christian word without Christ," added the pope, "leads you to vanity, to being sure of yourself, to pride, to power for power's sake. And the Lord lays such people low."

That truth, he explained, "is a constant in the history of salvation. Hannah, the mother of Samuel, says so; Mary says so in the Magnificat: the Lord puts down the vanity and pride of those who believe they are rocks." They are "people who run after a word, without Jesus Christ." They say a Christian word but "without Jesus Christ: without any relationship with Jesus Christ, without prayer with Jesus Christ; without service to Jesus Christ; without love for Jesus Christ."

For Pope Francis "what the Lord is telling us today" is an invitation "to build our life on that rock. And he is the rock. Paul says so explicitly," the pope made clear, "when he refers to that moment when Moses struck the rock with his staff. And he says: the rock was Christ. Christ is the rock." This meditation leads to "an examination of conscience," suggested the pope, "which will do us good." An "examination of conscience" that can be undertaken by answering a series of crucial questions. The pope spelled them out: "But what are our words like? Are the words enough in themselves? Are they words that think they are powerful? Are they words that think they can save us? Are they words with Jesus Christ? Is Jesus Christ always there when we say a Christian word?" And expressly referring again to "Christian words," the pope made a further point: "For when Jesus Christ isn't there, this also divides us from one another and creates divisions in the church."

Pope Francis concluded the homily by asking "the Lord for the grace to help us with this humility we should have: always to say Christian words in Jesus Christ, not without Jesus Christ." And he asked the Lord also to help us "in that humility to be disciples, who have been saved, and to go forward not with words that, because they feel themselves to be powerful, end up in the madness of vanity and the madness of pride." "May the Lord," he concluded, "give us the grace of humility to say words with Jesus Christ. Founded upon Jesus Christ."

The Annoying Cry

Friday, December 6, 2013
Isa 29:17-24; Mt 9:27-31

Prayer is "a cry" that's not afraid to "annoy God," to "make a noise." Like insistently "knocking at the door." That, according to Pope Francis, is the meaning of prayer addressed to the Lord in the spirit of truth and with the certainty that he can really grant it.

The pope spoke about this in his homily at the Mass celebrated on Friday morning, December 6, in the St. Martha's House chapel. Referring to the passage from Matthew chapter 9 (27-31), the pope began by calling our attention to a word in the gospel passage "that makes us think: cry." The blind who followed the Lord cried out to be cured. "And that blind man at the entrance to Jericho cried out too, and the Lord's friends tried to make him be quiet," the Holy Father recalled. But that man "asks the Lord for a grace and asks him by crying out loud," as if to say to Jesus: "But do it! It's my right that you should!"

"Here crying out is a sign of prayer," explained the pope. "When he taught us to pray, Jesus himself told us to do so like an annoying friend who came at midnight to ask for a bit of bread and some pasta for his guests." Or to "pray like the widow with the corrupt judge." Basically, continued the pope, "I'd call it praying by being annoying. I don't know. Perhaps that sounds wrong, but praying is rather like annoying God so that he will listen to us." And he added, the Lord himself said this, suggesting we should pray "like the friend at midnight, like the widow and the judge." So praying "is drawing the eyes, drawing the heart of God toward us." And that's just what the lepers in the gospel also did. They came to Jesus and told him: "But if you want to, you can cure us!" And "they did so feeling pretty sure."

"And that's how Jesus teaches us to pray," said the pope. Usually we present our requests to the Lord "once or twice or three times, but not that strongly; and then I get tired of asking and I forget to ask him anymore." Whereas the blind people in the passage from Matthew's gospel "cried out and wouldn't stop." In fact, the pope continued, "Jesus tells us: ask! He also tells us:

knock at the door! And someone knocking at the door disturbs, is a nuisance."

And "these are the very words Jesus uses to tell us how we should pray." But this is also "the way those in need pray whom we see in the gospel." Thus the blind "feel sure about asking the Lord to be cured," so that the Lord asks, "Do you believe I can do this?" And they reply: "Yes, Lord, we believe! We are sure!"

So here we have "the two attitudes of prayer," the pope continued. "It's both needy and sure." Prayer is "always needy. When we ask for something, prayer is needy: I need this, listen to me, Lord!" But "when it's true prayer, it's also sure: listen to me, I believe you can do this, because you promised!" In fact, explained the pope, "true Christian prayer is founded upon God's promise. He has promised."

The pope then referred to the first reading (Isaiah 29:17-21) in the day's liturgy, which contains God's promise of salvation to his people: "On that day the deaf shall hear the words of a scroll, and out of their gloom and darkness the eyes of the blind shall see." This passage, said the pope, "is a promise. It's all a promise, the promise of salvation: I will be with you, I will give you salvation!" And it's "with that certainty" that "we tell the Lord what we need. Certain that he can do it."

Besides, when we pray, it's the Lord himself who asks us: "Do you believe I can do this?" A question that leads on to the question each of us must ask ourselves: "Am I sure he can do it? Or do I pray a bit but don't feel sure he can do it?" The answer is that "he can do it," even if "we don't know when and how he will." That's precisely "what certainty of prayer means."

As for the specific "need" for which we pray, we have to present it "truly to the Lord: I'm blind, Lord, I have this need, I have this sickness, I have this sin, I have this pain." Thus "he hears our need and also hears that we are asking with certainty for his intervention."

In conclusion, Pope Francis repeated that we must pray always, "if our prayer is both needy and certain": it's "needy because we tell the truth to ourselves," and "certain because we believe that the Lord can do what we ask."

Holy Mass Concelebrated by Pope Francis with the
Patriarch of Alexandria of the Coptic Catholics,
His Beatitude Ibrahim Isaac Sidrak

Homily on the Occasion of the Celebration of Ecclesiastical Communion Granted to the Catholic Coptic Patriarch

Monday, December 9, 2013
Feast of the Immaculate Conception of the
Blessed Virgin Mary
Isa 35:1-10; Lk 5:17-26

Your Beatitude, Your Eminence,
Venerable brother bishops and priests,
Dear brothers and sisters,

For the first time as bishop of Rome I have the joy of welcoming a new patriarch, who has come to make a significant act of communion with the successor of Peter. Having accepted canonical election, Your Beatitude immediately asked for "ecclesiastical communion" with 'the church that presides in universal charity.' My venerable predecessor granted it willingly, mindful of the link with Peter's successor that the Catholic Coptic Church of Alexandria has always kept throughout its history. You are the expression of the preaching of St. Mark the evangelist: and that's the legacy he left you as a good interpreter of the apostle Peter.

In the first reading, the prophet Isaiah (cf. 35:1-10) reawakened in our hearts the expectation of the Lord's glorious return. We hear the encouragement to those who are "dismayed at heart," addressed to all those in your beloved land of Egypt who are experiencing insecurity and violence, sometimes on account of their Christian faith. "Courage! Don't be afraid!" Here are the comforting words that find confirmation in solidarity and fellowship. I'm grateful to God for this meeting, which gives me the opportunity to strengthen your hope and ours, because it's the same hope that "the burning sand shall become a pool, and the thirsty ground springs of water," and "the holy way" will be opened, the way of joy and happiness, "and sorrow and sighing shall flee away." That's our hope, the common hope of our two churches.

The gospel (Luke 5:17-26) shows us Christ overcoming human paralysis. It describes the power of divine mercy, which forgives sins and releases every sin when it encounters genuine faith. Moral paralysis is contagious. In complicity with historic poverty and our own sin, it can expand and become part of the social fabric and of communities till it blocks whole countries. But Christ's command can reverse the situation: "Stand up and walk!" Let us pray, trusting that in the Holy Land and the whole of the Middle East peace can always rise again from too frequent and sometimes dramatic setbacks. Let enmity and division come to an end. Let peace negotiations, which are often paralyzed by conflicting dark interests, quickly be resumed. Let real guarantees of religious freedom finally be given to all, together with the right of Christians to live quietly where they were born, in the country they love and have been citizens of for two thousand years, to go on contributing, as they always have, to the common good. May the Lord Jesus, who experienced flight into Egypt and was a guest in your generous land, watch over the Egyptians who are seeking dignity and security along the world's roads. And let us always go forward, seeking the Lord, seeking new roads, new ways to approach the Lord. And if it were necessary to make a hole in the roof to approach the Lord, may our kind and creative imagination lead us to do that: to finding and making a way to meet, a way to become brothers and sisters, a way of peace.

For our part, we want "to glorify God," changing dismay into amazement, for even today we can see "wonderful things." The wonder of the incarnation of the Word, and hence God's total closeness to humanity, which the mystery of Advent always brings home to us. May your great father Athanasius, set so close to the chair of Peter in the Vatican basilica, intercede for us, with St. Mark and St. Peter, and above all the immaculate and most holy mother of God. May they obtain for us from the Lord the joy of the gospel, granted in abundance to disciples and witnesses. Amen.

When God Re-Creates

Tuesday, December 10, 2013
Isa 40:1-11; Mt 18:12-14

Christians who lose hope lose the very meaning of their lives and it's as if they were up against a wall. Opening the doors to a meeting with the Lord means receiving from him that comfort which restores us with tenderness and hope. Pope Francis' homily, at the Mass celebrated on Tuesday morning, December 10, in St. Martha's chapel, was on that comforting tenderness by which the Lord re-creates hope in a Christian.

Quoting from the book of the prophet Isaiah (40:1-11), called "the Book of the Consolation of Israel," the pope focused on the comfort God brings his people. It's the Lord himself who "comes near to comfort them, give them peace." And thus "he does a

great work," because he "remakes all things, re-creates them."
This "re-creation," he added, is even more beautiful than creation.
So the Lord visits his people by "re-creating" them.

In fact the people of God were awaiting that visit; they knew
the Lord would come. "Let us remember," stressed the Holy Father, "Joseph's last words to his brothers: when the Lord visits
you, take my bones with you." Thus, he added, "the Lord will visit
his people. He is the hope of Israel. And he will visit them with
this comfort: re-creating everything. Not once, but many times."

The bishop of Rome described some aspects of this "re-creation." First, "when the Lord comes close to us, he gives us hope.
So," he said, "the Lord re-creates by hope. He always opens a
door." When the Lord approaches us, he doesn't shut doors but
opens them; and when he comes "he comes with open doors."

In Christian life this hope "is a real strength, it's a grace, it's
a gift." In fact, when "Christians lose hope their lives no longer
have any meaning. It's as if their life were up against a wall, nothing. But the Lord comforts us and re-creates us by hope, so that
we can go forward." He does so through a special closeness to
each one of us. In order to explain it the pope quoted the final
verse of the passage from Isaiah in the day's liturgy: "He will feed
his flock like a shepherd; he will gather the lambs in his arms, and
carry them in his bosom, and gently lead the mother sheep." And
he commented: "It's an image of tenderness. The Lord comforts
us with tenderness. The Lord, the great God, isn't afraid of tenderness. He becomes tenderness, becomes a baby, becomes little."
And "Jesus himself says so in the gospel: It's the Father's will that
not one of these little ones should be lost" (Matthew 18:12-14).
Because, explained the pope, "each of us is very, very important"
to the Lord, who makes us "walk on by giving us hope."

That "was Jesus' great work" during the forty days from the
resurrection to the ascension: "to comfort the disciples, come
close and give comfort, come close with tenderness. Think," said

the pope, "of the tenderness he showed to the apostles, to Mary Magdalene, to those on the road to Emmaus." And it's always like that. With us too. But we must ask the Lord for the grace "not to be afraid," he said in conclusion, "of the Lord's comforting, to be open, to ask for it, to seek it, because it's a comfort that gives us hope and will make us feel God the Father's tenderness."

When Silence Is Music

Thursday, December 12, 2013
Isa 41:13-20; Lk 1:26-38

Christmas is a festival when there's so much noise. But while we're going through this period of waiting it's important to rediscover silence, as the ideal moment to grasp the music of the language with which the Lord speaks to us. That language, said Pope Francis during the Mass celebrated on Thursday morning, December 12, in St. Martha's chapel, sounds very much like a father or mother: reassuring, full of love and tenderness.

As usual, the pope took his cue from the passage in the day's liturgy, taken from the book of the prophet Isaiah (41:13-20), which a few days before he had defined as "the Book of the Consolation of Israel," as he himself recalled. Pope Francis said he had reflected "not so much on what the Lord says" but on "how the Lord says it": that is, he explained a simile "not drawn from literature but, rather, from music."

How does the Lord speak? Perhaps, said the Holy Father, it might sound strange to hear a great God say: "I am the Lord your God, who holds your right hand, as a father holds his child's hand. And I say to you: Do not fear! I will help you." It's just like a father with his child, when the child has a bad dream at night

and his father says: "Don't be frightened. I'm here with you."
That's the way Jesus talks to us. He "comes close" to us. "When
we see a father or mother with their small child," explained the
bishop of Rome, "we see them becoming little; they speak in a
baby voice and act like babies." Someone watching from outside
might think they look rather silly. But "the father and mother's
love needs to get close," to "get down into the child's world." Even
if father or mother spoke normally the baby would understand;
"but they want to talk baby talk. They come close. They become
babies. And that's what the Lord is like."

Pope Francis recalled "the Greek theologians," who "in speaking of this used a very difficult word: *synkatabasis*, God's 'conde-
scension' (literally: 'going down with'), which makes him ready
to become one of us." That's the way the Lord speaks. He speaks
as parents do who say "rather silly things—my teddykin!—and
things like that." In fact, "Jesus also says: you little worm Jacob
(Isaiah 41:14), you're like a little worm to me, you're a tiny thing.
But I love you so." That's "the Lord's language: the language of
love, of a father or mother."

Of course, continued the pope, we must listen to the Lord's
words, to what he says to us; but we must also listen to "how he
says it." And we should do as he does, that is, "do what he says but
also do so in the way he says it: with love, with tenderness, 'going
down with' our brothers and sisters."

"I've always been struck," said the pope, "by the Lord's meeting with Elijah, when the Lord spoke with Elijah." It was on the
mountain and when Elijah saw him passing, "the Lord was not
in the hail, in the rain, the wind or the storm… The Lord was in
the still small voice" (cf. 1 Kings 19:11-13).

"The original," said the bishop of Rome, "uses a very beautiful word that can't be precisely translated: he was in a resonant
whisper of silence. A resonant whisper of silence—that's how the
Lord approaches, with that resonant silence that belongs to love."

And to everyone he says: "You are little, weak, a sinner. But I tell you I will make of you a threshing-sledge, sharp, new, and having teeth; you shall thresh the mountains and crush them and you shall make the hills like chaff. You shall winnow them and the wind shall carry them away, and the tempest shall scatter them." Thus he "makes himself small to make me powerful. He goes to his death in that 'going down,' so that I might live."

"This," said Pope Francis, "is the music of the Lord's language. In our preparation for Christmas we must listen to it. It will do us good, a lot of good." Usually Christmas is "a very noisy festival. It will do us good to have a bit of silence," to "hear those words of love, of closeness, those words of tenderness." And he concluded: "We must have silence at this time, so that, as the preface tell us, we may keep watch and wait."

WITHOUT FEAR OF FREEDOM

Friday, December 13, 2013
ISA 48:17-19; MT 11:16-19

There are some Christians who are "sort of allergic to preachers of the word": they accept "the truth of revelation" but not "the preacher," since they prefer "to live in a cage." It happened in Jesus' time and unfortunately it still happens today to those who live shut off in themselves, because they are afraid of the freedom that comes from the Holy Spirit.

For Pope Francis this was the teaching from the readings in the liturgy at the Mass celebrated on Friday morning, December 13, in St. Martha's chapel. The pope focused, in particular, on the passage from Matthew's gospel (11:16-19), in which Jesus compares his contemporaries' generation "to those children sitting in the market places and calling to one another, 'We played the flute for you and you did not dance, we wailed and you did not mourn.'"

The bishop of Rome recalled that in the gospel Christ "always speaks well of children," offering them as "a model of Christian life" and inviting us "to become like them in order to enter the kingdom of heaven." But, he noted, the passage in question "is the only time when he doesn't speak so well of them." For the pope we have here an image of children who are "a bit odd: rude, discontent, grumpy"; children who can't be happy while they are playing and "always refuse invitations from others: nothing suits them." In particular, Jesus uses this image to describe "the leaders of his people," whom the pope defined as "people who weren't open to God's word."

For the Holy Father there's an interesting thing about this attitude: their rejection, in fact, "isn't of the message, but the messenger." We have only to continue reading the gospel passage to confirm this. "For John came neither eating nor drinking and they say, 'He has a demon'; the Son of Man came eating and drinking, and they say, 'Look, a glutton and a drunkard, a friend of publicans and sinners.'" Actually, people have always found reasons to discredit the preacher. We have only to think of the people at that time who preferred "to take refuge in an elaborate religion: in moral precepts like the Pharisees; in political compromise like the Sadducees; in social revolution like the Zealots; in gnostic spirituality like the Essenes." All of them, he added, "with their tidy, well-made system," but which doesn't accept "the preacher." That's why Jesus refreshes their memory by reminding them of the prophets, who were persecuted and killed.

According to the pope, accepting "the truth of revelation" and "not the preacher" shows a mentality that comes from "living in a cage of precepts, or compromises, or revolutionary plans, or disembodied spirituality." Pope Francis referred in particular to those Christians "who won't dance when the preacher gives them good news of joy, and won't cry when the preacher gives them sad news." That is to say, those Christians "who are shut in, caged, who aren't free." And the reason for that is "fear of the freedom of the Holy Spirit, who comes through the preaching."

For "this is the scandal of the gospel about which St. Paul spoke; the scandal of preaching, which ends in the scandal of the cross." In fact, "it causes scandal that God speaks to us through human beings with limitations, sinful human beings; and it causes even more scandal that God speaks to us and saves us through a man who says he is the Son of God, but ends up as a criminal." For Pope Francis that's the way to block "the freedom that comes from the Holy Spirit," for ultimately "these sad Christians don't believe in the Holy Spirit; they don't believe in that freedom that comes from preaching, that warns you, teaches us, even slaps us, but which is the freedom that enables the church to grow."

So the gospel image of "the children who are afraid to dance or cry, who demand security in everything," makes us think "of those sad Christians, who always criticize preachers of truth, because they're afraid to open the door to the Holy Spirit." That's why the pope urged us to pray for them and always for ourselves, so that we "don't become sad Christians," Christians who deny "the Holy Spirit the freedom to come to us through the scandal of preaching."

THE MAN WHOSE EYE IS CLEAR

Monday, December 16, 2013
NUM 24:2-7, 15, 17A; MT 21:23-27

When prophecy is lacking, in comes clericalism to take its place, that rigid legalism that shuts the door in our face.

Hence the prayer in the lead-up to Christmas, that the spirit of prophecy may be heard among the people.

At the Mass celebrated on Monday morning, December 16, in St. Martha's chapel, Pope Francis reminded us that all the baptized are called to be prophets. He did so, as usual, by taking his cue from God's word in the day's liturgy. The pope repeated the words from the book of Numbers (24:2-7, 15-17b), which describe the figure of the prophet in "the oracle of Balaam son of Beor, the oracle of the man whose eye is clear, the oracle of one who hears the words of God." So here, he explained, "we have the prophet," a man "whose eye is clear and who hears the words of God, who can see into the moment and into the future. But first of all, he had heard the word of God."

And in fact "prophets have these three moments within them." First of all "the past: the prophet," said the Holy Father, "is aware of the promise and keeps God's promise in his heart, as a living word which he remembers and repeats." But "then he looks to the present, he looks at his people and feels the power of the spirit to say a word to help them stand up and continue the journey into the future."

So, the pope continued, "the prophet is a man of past, present, and future: the promise of the past, contemplation of the present, courage to show the road towards the future." And, he recalled, "the Lord has always safeguarded his people with prophets at difficult moments, moments when the people were discouraged or in disarray; when they had no temple; when Jerusalem was in the power of enemies; when the people were asking themselves: but Lord you promised us this and now what's happening?" And he added: "Perhaps the same thing happened in Mary's heart, when she stood at the foot of the cross: Lord, you told me this man would be the liberator of Israel, the leader who will bring us redemption; and now?"

"At that moment for the people of Israel," continued the pope, "it was necessary for a prophet to intervene. But the prophet wasn't always well received. Often he was rejected. Jesus himself told the Pharisees that their fathers had murdered the prophets because they said uncomfortable things, they told the truth, they remembered the promise." But, declared the pope, "when prophecy is lacking among the people of God, something else is lacking too: the life of the Lord is lacking."

For example, we have the story of the boy Samuel, "who heard the Lord's call while he was asleep, and didn't know what it was. And the Bible tells us: 'the word of the Lord was rare in those days, visions were not widespread'" (1 Samuel 3:1). It was a time when "Israel didn't have prophets." But, noted the bishop of Rome, "the same things happens when a prophet comes and the people don't accept him," as we read in the passage from Matthew's gospel (21:23-27).

"When there's no prophecy," he commented, "legalism steps in. And those priests went to Jesus to ask him about his legality: By what authority do you do these things?" It's as if they'd said: "We're the masters of the temple: by what authority do you do these things?" In fact, "they didn't understand the prophecies, they had forgotten the promise. They were unable to read the signs of the time; they didn't have clear eyes and were unable to hear the word of God. All they had was authority."

And "in Samuel's time, when the word of the Lord was rare and visions were not widespread, it was the same: legalism and authority." And that happened because "when there's no prophecy among the people, the space it leaves is taken over by clericalism. And it's that clericalism which demands of Jesus: by what authority do you do these things, what legality?"

Thus "memory of the promise and the hope of going forward are reduced to the present: losing its past and its hope for the future." It's as if in order to go forward all that matters is what is "present," what is "legal."

Of course, explained the pope, "perhaps the people of God who believed, who went to pray in the temple, wept in their hearts because they didn't find the Lord. Prophecy was lacking. They wept in their hearts as Hannah, Samuel's mother, wept, praying for fruitfulness for her people."

That fruitfulness, said the pope, "that comes from God's power, when he reawakens in us the memory of his promise and impels us toward the future in hope. That's the prophet. That's the man whose eye is clear and who hears the words of God."

Pope Francis concluded his homily by suggesting that we should offer "a prayer during these days when we're preparing for the Lord's birth." A prayer to the Lord that "prophets may not be lacking among your people. All we who have been baptized are prophets. Lord, may we not forget your promise; may we never tire of going forward, may we never shut ourselves off in the legality that closes doors. Lord, free your people from the spirit of clericalism and help them by the spirit of prophecy."

GOD'S SURNAME

Tuesday, December 17, 2013
GEN 49:2, 8-10; MT 1:1-17

God's surname is human. In fact the Lord takes on the name of each one of us, whether we are saints or sinners, to make it his own surname. For by becoming incarnate the Lord made history with humanity; it was his joy to share his life with us "and that's enough to make us weep: so much love, so much tenderness."

It was with that thought about Christmas soon to come that

Pope Francis commented on Tuesday, December 17, on the two readings from the day's liturgy of the word, taken respectively from Genesis (49:2, 8-10) and from Matthew's gospel (1:1-17). On the day of his seventy-seventh birthday the Holy Father presided as usual at the morning Mass in St. Martha's chapel. Concelebrating with him, among others, was the cardinal dean of the College of Cardinals, Angelo Sodano, who passed on the good wishes of the whole college.

In his homily on God's presence in human history, the bishop of Rome picked out two terms, heredity and genealogy, as the keys to interpreting, respectively, the first reading—about Jacob's prophecy when he gathered his sons and foretold a glorious progeny for Judah—and the gospel passage containing the genealogy of Jesus. Focusing in particular on the latter, he stressed that this was "not a telephone book" but "an important account: it's pure history," because "God sent his Son" among human beings. And, he added, "Jesus is consubstantial with the Father, God; but also consubstantial with his mother, a woman. And his consubstantiality with his mother means this: God entered history; God wanted to become part of history. With us. He walked through life with us."

It was a road, the bishop of Rome continued, that began long ago, in Paradise, immediately after the original sin. From that moment, the Lord "had this idea: to walk through life with us." So "he called Abraham, the first name on this list and invited him to get going. And Abraham began on that road: he begat Isaac and Isaac begat Jacob and Jacob begat Judah." And so on, through the history of humanity. So "God walks with his people," because "he didn't want to come and save us outside history; he wanted to become part of history with us." A history, said the pope, consisting of holiness and sin, for in the list of Jesus' genealogy there are saints and sinners. Among the earliest, the pope recalled, were "our father Abraham" and "David who after his sin repented." Among the later names there were "sinners who committed grave sins," but with whom God also "made history." Sinners who didn't know how to respond to the project God had planned for them: like "Solomon, who was so great and intelligent, but who ended up as a poor wretch who didn't even know his own name." However, declared Pope Francis, God was also with him. "And that's what's so beautiful: God makes history with us. And furthermore, when God wants to say who he is, he says, I am the God of Abraham, Isaac, and Jacob."

So that's why, said Pope Francis to the question "what is God's surname?" we can answer: "We are, each of us. He takes our name to make it his surname." And in the example given by the pope there are not only the fathers of our faith, but also common people. "I am the God of Abraham, Isaac, Jacob, Peter, Marietta, Armony, Marisa, Simon, of everyone. He takes his surname from us. God's surname is each of us," he explained.

So we see that by taking "our name as his surname, God made history with us." What's more, "he let us write the story." And today we still continue to write "this story," which is made up of "grace and sin," while the Lord never tires of staying with us. "That's God's humility, God's patience, God's love." And even "the book of Samuel tells us that the joy of the Lord is among the children of humanity, with us."

So now that "Christmas is coming," it came naturally to Pope Francis—as he himself confided in concluding his reflection—to think, "If he made his own history with us, if he took his surname from us, if he allowed us to write his story," we should allow God to write our story. For, he explained, "holiness" means "letting the Lord write our story." And that was the pope's Christmas wish "for all of us." A wish that was an invitation to open our hearts: "May the Lord write your story and may you let him do so."

Trying to Save Ourselves on Our Own

Thursday, December 19, 2013
Jud 13:2-7, 24-25a; Lk 1:5-25

We can't save ourselves on our own and anyone who has tried, even among Christians, has failed. For only God can give life and salvation. This was Pope Francis' Advent meditation during the Mass celebrated this Thursday morning, December 19, in the chapel of St. Martha's House.

Taking his cue, as usual, from the day's liturgy, the pope reminded us that "life, the ability to give life and salvation come from the Lord alone" and not from human beings, who don't have "the humility" to recognize that and ask for help. "So often" in the Bible we hear about "a barren woman, infertility, the inability to conceive and give life." But very often too there is "the Lord's miracle, which enables these barren women to have a child."

First of all, Pope Francis mentioned Samson's mother, whose story was read this morning in the passage from the book of Judges (13:2-7, 24-25a). And then he also recalled what "happened to the wife of our father Abraham: she couldn't believe" she would have a child because of her advanced age; and "she laughed at the entrance to the tent, where she stood listening to what her husband was talking about. She laughed because she couldn't believe it. But she had a son." Today's gospel (Luke 1:5-25), continued the pope, also tells us "what happened to Elizabeth." These, he said, are all biblical stories of women that show how "life comes out of a situation from which it's impossible for it to come." And it also happened to women who weren't barren but who no longer had any hope in their lives. "Think about Naomi," said the bishop of Rome, "who ended up having a grandson." Basically, "the Lord intervenes in the lives of these women to tell us: I am able to give life!"

Pope Francis noted that in the words of "the prophets there's the image of the desert, which can't bring forth a tree, a fruit or sprout anything." Nevertheless, "the desert will be like a forest. The prophets tell us: it will be great, it will flower!" So "the desert can flower" and "the barren woman can produce life," only because of "the Lord's promise: I can! I can make life and salvation grow out of your dryness! I can make barrenness bear fruit!" Salvation is "God's intervention that makes us fruitful, that enables us to give life," that "helps us on the way to holiness."

One thing is certain: "We can't save ourselves on our own." This has been proved so often even among "some Christians," the pope recalled, mentioning the Pelagians. But it's only God's intervention that brings us salvation.

So then the pope asked: "So what about us? What must we do?" First of all, Pope Francis answered, "recognize our barrenness, our inability to give life." Then "ask." And he formulated our request as a prayer: "Lord, I want to be fruitful; I want my life to give life, my faith to be fruitful and go forward and give it to others. Lord, I'm barren; I can't, you can. I'm a desert; I can't, you can." And his wish was: "Let that be our prayer in these days before Christmas."

It makes us think, the pope continued, "how the proud, those who believe they can do everything by themselves, are struck down." And he referred in particular to "that woman who wasn't barren, but she was proud and didn't understand what it meant to praise God: Michal, daughter of Saul. She laughed at praise. And she was punished with barrenness." Humility is a necessary quality in order to be fruitful. "So many people," he remarked, "think they're fine, as she did, and in the end they become miserable wretches!"

But what's important is "the humility to say, 'Lord, I am barren, I'm a desert.'" And how important it is during these days to repeat "the beautiful O antiphons which pray: O Son of David,

O Adonai, O Wisdom—today—O Root of Jesse, O Emmanuel, come and give us life, come and save us because you alone can do so; I can't on my own."

So, concluded the pope, "with that humility, the humility of the desert, the humility of a barren soul," we "need grace, the grace to flower, bear fruit, and give life."

MYSTERY DOESN'T SEEK PUBLICITY

Friday, December 20, 2013
ISA 7:10-14; LK 1:26-38

The mystery of God's relationship with human beings doesn't seek publicity, because that wouldn't make it truthful. It needs silence. It's up to each one of us to discover, in silence, the ways of God's mystery in our personal life. With a few days till Christmas, Pope Francis offered a powerful reflection on the value of silence. And he invited us to love it and seek it as Mary did, about whom we heard during the Mass celebrated this morning, Friday, December 20, in the chapel of St. Martha's House.

The pope's reflection was based on the passage from Luke's gospel in today's liturgy (1:26-38), beginning with "that sentence," which "tells us so much," addressed to Mary by the angel: "The power of the Most High will overshadow you. The Holy Spirit will come upon you." This also recalls the passage from the book of Isaiah (7:10-14), proclaimed in the first reading of the Mass.

"It's God's shadow," explained the pope, "which always guards the mystery in the history of salvation." It was "God's shadow that accompanied his people in the wilderness." The whole history of salvation shows that "the Lord has always taken care of the mystery. He has covered up the mystery. He hasn't given it publicity." In fact, "the mystery that goes in for publicity isn't Christian, it's not God's mystery. It's a fake mystery." Today's gospel passage confirms that, continued the pope. When Mary hears from the angel that she will have a son, "the mystery of her motherhood" remains hidden.

And this goes for us too. "That shadow of God in us, in our life," said the pope, helps us "to discover our own mystery: the mystery of our meeting with the Lord, the mystery of our way through life with the Lord." In fact "each of us," the pope explained, "knows how the Lord works mysteriously in our heart and soul. And what is the cloud, the power, the way of the Holy Spirit to cover our mystery? That cloud in us, in our life, is called silence. Silence is the cloud that covers the mystery of our relationship with the Lord, of our holiness and our sins."

"It's a mystery," he continued, "that we can't explain. But when there's no silence in our life, the mystery is lost, it goes away." So that's why it's so important "to guard the mystery by silence: that's the cloud, that's God's power in us, that's the power of the Holy Spirit."

Pope Francis then returned to Mary's witness, who lived with "this silence" all her life long. "I think," said the pope, "of how often she kept silence, how often she didn't say what she was feeling in order to guard the mystery of her relationship with her son." And he recalled: "In 1964 at Nazareth Paul VI told us that all of us need to renew, strengthen, and refresh that silence," because "silence guards the mystery." The pope then spoke about "Mary's silence at the foot of the cross," and what went through her mind, and reminded us that John Paul II had also spoken about it.

In fact, he said, "the gospel doesn't report a word uttered by Mary at the foot of the cross: she "was silent, but within her heart how many things she said to the Lord" at that crucial time. Probably, Mary remembered the angel's words, which "we heard read" in the gospel about her son: "On that day you told me he would be great! You told me he would be given the throne of his father David and reign forever! But look at him now," on the cross. "By her silence she covered up the mystery she didn't understand. And by her silence she allowed the mystery to grow and flower," bringing "great hope" to all.

"The Holy Spirit will come upon you, the power of the Most High will overshadow you": the angel's words to Mary, said the pope again, assure us that "the Lord covers up his mystery." Because "the mystery of our relationship with God, our walk through life, our salvation can't be brought out into the open, advertised. Silence guards it." Pope Francis concluded his homily with the prayer that "the Lord may give us all the grace to love silence, to seek it, to have a heart guarded by the cloud of silence. And thus the mystery growing within us will bear many fruits."

WAITING FOR THE BIRTH

Monday, December 23, 2013
MAL 3:1-4, 23-24; LK 1:57-66

At Christmas we experience "the feelings of a woman waiting to give birth." This is a spiritual attitude requiring "openness," so we must never pin "a polite notice" on the door of our soul saying: "Please Do Not Disturb."

Pope Francis spoke powerfully about the true meaning of Christmas during the Mass celebrated on Monday, December 23, in St. Martha's chapel. "During this last week" before Christmas, the pope recalled, "the church repeats the prayer: Come, Lord!" And in doing so, "she calls upon him using many different names, which are charged with a message about the Lord" himself: "O

Wisdom, O Root of Jesse, O Sun, O King of Nations, O Emmanuel today."

The church does this, explained the Holy Father, because "she's waiting for a birth." In fact, "during this week, the church is like Mary: waiting for the birth." In her heart Mary "felt what all women feel at that time": something special, that "feeling in her body and soul" which makes her realize her child is about to be born. And in her heart surely she said to the child in her womb: "Come, I want to see your face, because they told me you would be great!"

In fact, "the Lord comes twice." His first coming, explained the bishop of Rome, is "the one we're commemorating now, his physical birth." Then "he will come at the end, to finish the story." But, he added, "St. Bernard tells us that there's a third coming of the Lord: his coming every day." Actually, "the Lord visits his church every day. He visits each one of us. And there is a likeness: our soul is like the church; our soul is like Mary." Pope Francis recalled that "the desert fathers said Mary, the church, and our soul are all feminine." So "what is said about one of them can be said analogously about the other."

So "our soul is in waiting, waiting for the Lord to come. An open soul cries: Come, Lord!" During these days, the pope reiterated, the Holy Spirit moves the heart of each one of us to "offer this prayer: come, come!" Besides, "all through Advent," he recalled, "we have been saying in the preface that we, the church, like Mary, are "waiting in watch." And "watchfulness is the virtue, the attitude of pilgrims. We're pilgrims." And this prompted the pope to ask: "Are we waiting or are we closed in? Are we watchful or are we shut up snugly in a wayside inn and not going any further? Are we pilgrims or drifters?"

That's why the church invites us to pray saying: "Come!" It means "opening up our soul" so that during these days it "keeps watch and waits." It's an invitation to understand "what's happening" within us: "whether the Lord comes or doesn't come; whether there's room for the Lord or only room for feasting, celebrating, making a noise." And according to the pope, that leads to another question to ask ourselves: "Is our soul open, as holy mother church is open, and as Mary was? Or is our soul closed and have we pinned on its door a very polite notice saying: Please Do Not Disturb?"

"The world doesn't end with us," the pope went on, and "we aren't more important than the world." So, he continued, "with Mary and with mother church it will do us good to repeat these invocations today in prayer: O Wisdom, O Key of David, O King of Nations, come, come!" And, he insisted, it will do us good to "repeat over and over: come!" A prayer which becomes an examination of conscience to discover "how our soul is" and make sure "it isn't a soul that tells" other people it doesn't want to be disturbed. Rather, let it be "a soul that is open, a great soul to receive the Lord during these days." A soul, concluded the Holy Father, "that begins to feel what the church will tell us tomorrow in the antiphon: know that the Lord is coming today and tomorrow you will see his glory."

A Heart Like a Market Place

Monday, January 6, 2014
1 Jn 3:22–4:6; Mt 4:12, 22-25

The human heart is like "a local market," where you can find everything. Christians should learn to know thoroughly what goes on in it, discerning what flows the way pointed by Christ and what leads the other way pointed by the antichrist. In his homily during the Mass celebrated on Monday morning,

January 6, in St. Martha's chapel, Pope Francis told us the criterion by which to judge this is to follow the route indicated by the incarnation of the Word.

The pope offered this reflection while commenting on the first letter of John (3:22–4:6), in which the apostle "almost obsessively" repeats certain words of advice, in particular: "Abide in the Lord."

"Abide in the Lord," repeated the pope, adding, "The Christian man or woman is someone who abides in the Lord." But what does this mean? So many things, replied the Holy Father. However, he explained, the passage from John's letter focuses on a particular attitude Christians should adopt if they want to abide in the Lord: "that is, being fully aware of what is going on in their hearts."

Christians who abide in the Lord know "what's happening in their hearts." That's why the apostle "says: 'Beloved, do not believe every spirit, but test the spirits'; know how to discern the spirits; know what you feel, what you think, what you want, if it's to abide in the Lord or something else that will distance you from the Lord." For "our hearts," continued the pope, "always have desires, wishes, and thoughts: but are all these from the Lord? Or do some of them distance us from the Lord? That's why the apostle says: test everything you think, feel, want… If it's in line with the Lord, that's fine; but if it isn't…"

So it's necessary "to test the spirits," repeated the bishop of Rome, quoting again from John's letter, "'to see whether they are from God; for many false prophets have gone out into the world.'" And not only the prophets themselves may be false, but also their prophecies, what they say. So it's necessary always to be on the watch. So, the pope insisted, the Christian man or woman is someone who "knows how to keep watch over their heart."

A heart, added Pope Francis, in which there are "so many things that come and go … It's like a local market in which you can find anything." For that very reason we need to keep discerning, in order to realize, said the pope, what is truly from the Lord.

But "how do I know," he asked, "that this is from Christ?" The apostle John gives us the clue. And the Holy Father reminded us of it by quoting again from the letter: "Every spirit that confesses that Jesus Christ has come in the flesh is from God, and every spirit that does not confess Jesus is not from God. And this is the spirit of the antichrist, of which you have heard that it's coming; and now it's already in the world."

"It's that simple: if something you want or something you think," he explained, "is in line with the incarnation of the Word, the Lord who came in the flesh," it means that it's from God, but if it isn't, then it doesn't come from God. So basically, we have to recognize the way taken by God, who "lowered himself, humiliated himself, to death on the cross." Lowering yourself, humility, and also humiliation: "that," said the pope, "is the way of Jesus Christ."

So if a thought or a wish "takes you the way of humility, lowering yourself, serving others, it's from Jesus; but if it leads you to self-sufficiency, vanity, pride, or along the way of abstract thought, it isn't from Jesus." Witness the temptations that Jesus himself underwent in the wilderness. "All three suggestions by which the devil tempted Jesus were suggestions not to go that way, the way of service, humility, humiliation, charity."

"Let us think about this today," said the pope. "It will do us good. First: what's happening in my heart? What am I thinking? What am I feeling? Do I pay attention, or do I let everything come and go? Do I know what I want? Do I test what I want, what I desire? Or do I take everything? Beloved, do not believe every spirit, but test the spirits." So often, he added, our heart "is like a street where everyone goes by." But for that very reason it's necessary to "test" and to ask ourselves "if we always choose the things that come from God, if we know what are the things that come from God, if we know the true criterion for discerning" our desires, our thoughts. And, he concluded, we must never forget "the true criterion is God's incarnation."

Love Isn't a Soap Opera

Wednesday, January 8, 2014
1 Jn 4:11-18; Mk 6:45-52

True love isn't like a soap opera. It doesn't consist of illusions. True love is palpable and practical, based on deeds, not words; on giving, not seeking advantages. The spiritual recipe for loving deeply lies in the word "abide," a "double abiding: we in God and God in us." In the Mass celebrated in the chapel of St. Martha's House on Wednesday morning, January 8, Pope Francis pointed to true love's one foundation in the person of Jesus Christ, God's Word made man. This truth, he said, is "the key to Christian life," "the criterion" of love.

As usual, the pope took his cue for his meditation from the day's liturgy, in particular, from the first reading (1 John 4:11-18), where the decisive word "abide" occurs several times. The apostle John, said the pope, "tells us so many times that we must abide in the Lord. And he also tells us that the Lord abides in us." Basically, he says "Christian life is this 'abiding.' This double abiding: we in God and God in us." But "not abiding in the spirit of the world. Not abiding in superficiality, not abiding in idolatry, not abiding in vanity. No, abiding in the Lord!" And, explained the pope, the Lord "returns this" and so "he too abides in us." Or rather "he first abides in us" but "we so often chase him away" and so "we can't abide in him."

"Those who abide in love abide in God and God abides in them," John continues, telling us, said the pope, that in practice "abiding in God is the same as abiding in love." And "it's a beautiful thing to hear that about love!" he added, but also warned: "But be aware that the love John is speaking of isn't love like in a soap opera! No, it's something else!" Actually, explained the pope, "Christian love always has a certain quality: embodiment. Christian love is palpable and practical. When Jesus himself speaks of love, he speaks about palpable, practical things: feeding the hungry, visiting the sick." These are all "practical things," because "love is palpable and practical." That's "Christian practicality."

So Pope Francis warned that "when that practicality is lacking," we end up "with a disembodied Christianity based on illusions, because we fail to understand the central message of Jesus." Love that isn't "palpable and practical" becomes "love based on illusions." It was also an "illusion" which "the disciples had when they saw Jesus and thought he was a ghost," as we read in the gospel passage from Mark (6:45-52). But, the pope commented, "Love based on illusions, that isn't palpable and practical, doesn't do us any good."

"But when does this happen?" asked the pope to understand how we fall into disembodied illusions. The answer, he said, is given very clearly in the gospel. When the disciples thought they were seeing a ghost, explained the pope, quoting the text, "they were utterly astounded, for they did not understand about the loaves but their hearts were hardened." And "if your heart is hardened, you can't love. And you think love means imagining things. No, love is palpable and practical!" That's a fundamental criterion for loving truly. "The criterion of abiding in the Lord and the Lord in us," said the pope, "and the criterion of Christian embodied practicality is always the same: the Word became flesh." The criterion is faith in "the incarnation of the Word, God become man." And "there's no true Christianity without this foundation. The key to Christian life is faith in Jesus Christ, God's Word become human."

Pope Francis also suggested the way to "know" what palpable, practical love means. He explained that "there are some consequences to this criterion." He mentioned two. The first was that "love lies more in deeds than words. Jesus himself said so: it's not those who say to me 'Lord, Lord,' who talk this way, who will enter the kingdom of heaven, but those who do God's will." So the invitation is to be "practical" doing "God's works."

There's a question each of us must ask ourselves: "If I abide in

Jesus, abide in the Lord, abide in love, what do I do—not what do I think or what do I say—for God, or what do I do for others?" So "the first criterion is to love by deeds, not words." For words "are blown away on the wind: they're here today and gone tomorrow."

The "second criterion for being palpable and practical" proposed by the pope "is that in loving it's more important to give than to receive." People "who love give—give things, give life, give themselves to God and to others," whereas people "who don't love and are selfish always want to receive. They always want to get things, get advantages." So that's the spiritual advice: "keep an open heart, not like the disciples whose hearts were closed," so they didn't understand. It means, the pope declared again, "abiding in God" so that "God abides in us. And abiding in love."

The one and only "criterion for abiding is our faith in Jesus Christ, God's Word made flesh: the mystery we're celebrating at this time." And then he said again: "The two consequences of this Christian practicality, the criterion, are that love lies more in deeds than words; and love lies more in giving than receiving."

"Looking at the Baby, during these three last days of Christmas time, looking at the Word made flesh," Pope Francis concluded his homily by inviting us to renew "our faith in Jesus Christ, true God and true man. And let us ask him for the grace of this palpable, practical Christian love, so that we may always abide in love," in such a way "that he may abide in us."

PARROTING THE CREED
Thursday, January 9, 2014
1 Jn 4:19–5:4; Lk 4:14–22

Christians don't repeat the Creed by heart like parrots and live as if they are always "defeated." They confess their faith entirely and are capable of worshiping God, thereby raising the temperature of the church's life. For Pope Francis "confessing and trusting" are the two key words that nourish and strengthen the believer's attitude, because "our faith is the victory that has conquered the world," as the apostle John writes in his first letter. The pope repeated this at the Mass celebrated on Thursday morning, January 9, in the chapel of St. Martha's House.

Pope Francis took up the thread of the previous day's meditation, and continued his reflection based on John's first letter, which, he explained, "insistently stresses the word that for him is the expression of Christian life: abide, abiding in the Lord." And "during these days," he continued, "we've seen how" John "thinks of this abiding: we in the Lord and the Lord in us. That means abiding in love, because the two principal commandments are loving God and loving our neighbor."

So for John, the center of Christian life is "abiding in the Lord, and the Lord abiding in us, abiding in love. That's why we've been given the Spirit, he says. It's the Holy Spirit that accomplishes this work of abiding." In the passage from his first letter (4:19–5:4), read in the liturgy, noted the pope, the apostle answers a question that comes naturally to us: what do we have to do for this "abiding"? John writes: Everyone who abides in God, everyone who has been born of God, everyone who abides in love conquers the world. "And that victory is our faith," explained the pope, repeating the apostle's words. For "this abiding," he repeated, "on our part" there's faith, whereas "for God's part there's the Holy Spirit who accomplishes this work of grace."

"It's powerful!" exclaimed the pope, "because the victory that has conquered the world is our faith. Our faith can do anything; it's victorious!" This is a truth that "it would be lovely" to tell ourselves often, "because so often we're defeated Christians, who don't believe faith is a victory, who don't live by this faith. And if we don't live by this faith we're defeated. The world conquers, the prince of this world."

So the fundamental question to ask ourselves is: "What is this faith?" Pope Francis recalled how Jesus spoke of faith and showed its power, as we see in the gospel stories of the woman with a hemorrhage, the Canaanite woman, or the man who came to Jesus with faith to ask to be healed—Jesus told him: "Great is your faith!"—or the man born blind. The Lord, recalled the pope, "also said that anyone who had faith like a grain of mustard seed can move mountains."

And "this faith asks two things of us: to confess and to trust," said the pope. First of all "faith is confessing God, but the God who revealed himself to us from the time of our fathers up till now, the God of history." That's what we declare every day in the Creed. But, the pope made clear, "it's one thing to say the Creed from your heart and another to parrot it: I believe in God, I believe in Jesus Christ, I believe..." The pope went on to suggest an examination of conscience: "Do I believe in what I say? Is this confession of faith true or do I say it from memory because it has to be said? Or do I only half believe?"

So we must "confess the faith." And confess "it all, not just part of it!" But, he added, "we must also "keep it all as it has been handed down to us by tradition. The whole faith!" The pope then gave the "sign" by which we can "recognize the faith properly." Actually, "anyone who confesses the faith properly, the whole faith, is capable of worshiping God." It's a sign that may seem "a bit strange," commented the pope, "because we know how to ask God for things, how to thank God. But worshiping God, praising God is something more. Only someone who has this strong faith is able to worship."

In worshiping, the pope noted, "I dare say that the temperature of the church is a bit low: we Christians don't have a great capacity for worship—although some do—because in our confession of faith we aren't convinced. Or we're half convinced." But we need to recover the capacity "to praise, to worship" God; also because, added the pope, "we all pray to ask for things and to thank God."

As for the second attitude, Pope Francis recalled how "the man or woman who has faith trusts in God. They trust. At a dark moment in his life Paul said: I know the one in whom I have trusted. God. The Lord Jesus." And trust, said the pope, "leads us to hope. Just as the confession of faith leads us to worship and praise God, trusting in God leads us to an attitude of hope."

But, the pope warned, "there are so many Christians with a watered-down hope," a watered-down hope that isn't "strong." And what's the reason for his "weak hope"? Of course it's the lack "of the strength and courage to trust in the Lord." But to be "victorious Christians," he stressed, we must believe "confessing the faith and also keeping the faith, and trusting in God, the Lord." That's the victory that has conquered the world: our faith.

"To abide in the Lord, abide in love," he repeated, "we need the Holy Spirit, from God. But what's needed from us is confessing the faith, which is a gift, and trusting in the Lord Jesus, in order to worship, praise, and have hope." Pope Francis concluded his homily with the prayer that "the Lord may make us able to understand and live by that beautiful saying" of the apostle John read in the liturgy: "And this is the victory that has conquered the world: our faith."

What a Priest Should Be Like

Friday, January 10, 2014
1 Jn 5:5-13; Lk 5:12-16

It's "his relationship with Jesus Christ" that saves the priest from the temptation of worldliness, the risk of becoming smoothly "unctuous" rather than "anointed," the risk of idolatry of "the God Narcissus." Indeed, the priest can "lose everything" but not his bond with the Lord; otherwise he wouldn't have anything to offer his people. With strong words and proposing a true examination of conscience, Pope Francis directly addressed priests on the value of their anointing. He did so in his homily at the Mass celebrated on Friday morning, January 10, in the chapel of St. Martha's House.

The pope continued his meditation on the first letter of John, which he had begun in recent days. The passage in the day's liturgy (5:5-13), he explained, "tells us that we have eternal life because we believe in the name of Jesus." Here are the apostle's words: "I write these things to you who believe in the name of the Son of God, so that you may know you have eternal life."

This is "the development of the verse" read in Friday's liturgy, on which the pope had focused his previous meditation: "And this is the victory that conquers the world: our faith." In fact, the pope confirmed, "our faith is a victory against the spirit of the world. Our faith is this victory that makes us go forward in the name of the Son of God, the name of Jesus."

This reflection led the Holy Father to ask a decisive question: what is our relationship with Jesus like? A truly fundamental question, "our victory is made strong in our relationship with Jesus." A "tough" question, he admitted, especially "for us who are priests: what is my relationship like with Jesus Christ?"

"A priest's strength," the pope reminded us, "lies in this relationship." In fact, when "his popularity was growing, Jesus went to his Father." In the gospel passage in today's liturgy, Luke (5:12-16) tells us: "But he would withdraw to deserted places and pray." So "when there was more and more talk" of Jesus, "and many crowds would gather to hear him and be cured of their diseases, afterwards Jesus went to find his Father." An attitude, said the pope, "that is the touchstone for us priests: do we or don't we go to find Jesus?"

From this flowed a series of questions that the pope suggested for an examination of conscience: "What place has Jesus Christ in my life as a priest? Is it a living relationship of disciple with master, brother with brother, poor human being with God? Or is it a rather artificial relationship that doesn't come from the heart?"

"We're anointed by the spirit," the pope reflected, "and when a priest distances himself from Jesus Christ, instead of being anointed, he ends up being smoothly unctuous." And, noted the pope, "what a lot of harm these smooth priests do the church! Those who put their strength into artificial things, into vanities," those who "behave and talk in an affected, simpering way." And how often, he added, "we hear it said with pain: but this is a priest who's more like a 'butterfly,' because 'he's vain' and doesn't have a relationship with Jesus Christ: he's lost his anointing; he's become smoothly unctuous."

Even with all our limitations, "we're good priests," continued the pope, "if we go to Jesus Christ, if we seek the Lord in prayer: prayer of intercession, prayer of worship." But if "we distance ourselves from Jesus Christ, we complement this with other worldly attitudes." And so we get "all those types" like "the profiteering priest, the priest entrepreneur." But, he declared forcefully, the priest "worships Jesus Christ, the priest talks with Jesus Christ, the priest seeks Jesus Christ and lets Jesus Christ seek him. That's the heart of our lives. If that's lacking we lose everything! And what will we have to give the people?"

So the bishop of Rome repeated the prayer in the day's collect: "We asked," he said, "that the mystery that we are celebrating, the Word become flesh among us in Jesus Christ, might grow every day. We asked for this grace: that our relationship with Jesus Christ, the relationship of those anointed for his people, might grow stronger in us."

"It's lovely to find priests," the pope remarked, "who have

given their lives as priests." Priests about whom people say, "Yes, he's quite a character, he's got this and that, but he's a priest! And the people have a nose for that!" But if, on the other hand, we find priests who are, to put it bluntly, "idolatrous," who instead of having Jesus have little idols—some are devoted to the god Narcissus—when the people see that they say: "poor devils!" So it's "our relationship with Jesus Christ," declared the pope, that saves us "from worldliness, and the idolatry that makes us smoothly unctuous" and that keeps us to our "anointing."

Finally, turning to those present—among whom were a group of priests from Genoa with Cardinal Archbishop Angelo Bagnasco—Pope Francis concluded his homily thus: "Today for you, who have kindly come to concelebrate here with me, I wish this: lose everything in life but don't lose your relationship with Jesus Christ. That's your victory. And onward with that!"

TAILOR-MADE LOVE

Monday, January 13, 2014
1 SAM 1:1-8; MK 1:14-20

God prepares the way for each of us. He does so with love, a love that is "tailor-made," because he prepares it for each of us personally. And he's ready to intervene from time to time and straighten us out, just as a mother and father do. This was Pope Francis' reflection on Monday morning, January 13, during the Mass celebrated in St. Martha's chapel.

The pope took his cue from the episode in Mark's gospel (1:14-20) when, after John's arrest, Jesus went to Galilee, giving the impression he wanted to start on another stage of his course.

"And he proclaims the gospel," noted the pope, "with the same words as those used by John: 'The time is fulfilled and the kingdom of God has come near, repent.' Jesus says the same as John said. John had prepared the way for Jesus. And Jesus follows it."

"Preparing the ways, also preparing our lives, is what God does, what God's love does for each of us," explained the bishop of Rome. "He doesn't make us Christians by spontaneous generation," the pope continued. "He prepares our way, prepares our life, for a good while." And referring to the gospel passage, he added, "It seems that Simon, Andrew, James, and John were definitively chosen"; but that doesn't mean that from then on they were "definitively faithful." In fact, they made mistakes: they made "unchristian proposals to the Lord"; they actually denied him. Peter more than the rest. They got frightened, explained the pope, and they "went astray, they forsook the Lord."

It's a work of preparation that Jesus has been doing for generations. And to confirm this the pope referred to Hannah, the second wife of Elkanah, quoted in the first reading of the liturgy (cf. 1 Samuel 1:1-8). This woman, who was "barren and wept" when his other wife, Peninnah, who had children, mocked her. But Hannah's weeping was preparation for the birth of the great Samuel. "Thus the Lord," declared the pope, "prepares us over many generations. And when things don't go well, he becomes involved in history" and sorts it out. In Jesus' own genealogy, he recalled, "there are sinners. Both men and women. But what did the Lord do? He became involved; he straightened things out; he put things right. Think of the great David, a great sinner and then a great saint. The Lord knows that. When the Lord tells us: with everlasting love I have loved you so much, he's referring to that. For generations the Lord has been thinking 'about us.'" And so he accompanies us, feeling our own feelings, when he is there at the marriage, when a child is expected—at every moment of our life "he accompanies and takes care of us."

"That," the pope confirmed, "is the Lord's everlasting love. Everlasting but palpable and practical. And his love is tailor-made for each of us, because he creates the history and prepares the way for each of us. That's God's love." Then the pope turned to a group of priests who were concelebrating on the occasion of the sixtieth anniversary of their ordination and said: "You're thinking about your sixty years of saying Mass. What a lot of things have happened. Such a lot! The Lord was there preparing the way, for other people as well, whom we don't know, but he knows them." He is "the Lord of preparation, who has always loved us and never forsakes us." Perhaps, he admitted, "it's a difficult act of faith to believe this; that's true. Because our rationalism makes us say: with all the people he is concerned with, why should the Lord think about me?" And yet he "has prepared the way for me, with our mothers, our grandmothers, our fathers, our grandfathers, and great grandparents, all of them: that's what the Lord does. And that's how his love is: palpable and practical, everlasting and also tailor-made."

"Let us pray," he concluded, "by asking for the grace to understand God's love. But it can never be grasped, can it? It can be felt, it can be wept over, but it can't be grasped. And this also tells us how great that love is."

FOUR MODELS

Tuesday, January 14, 2014
1 SAM 1:9-20; MK 1:21B-28

People follow anyone who teaches like Jesus, who brings the newness of God's word, his love. And not someone—whether they are laity, priest, or bishop—who is corrupt and has a corrupt heart. Pope Francis spoke again of the witness to the faith that should be borne by those, particularly those, who have been given the mission, who have been called to pass it on to the people of God. And during the homily at the Mass celebrated this morning, Tuesday, January 14, in St. Martha's chapel, he repeated that there's no other way than the one taught by Christ.

That teaching is referred to in both the readings for the day's liturgy, taken from the first book of Samuel (1:9-20) and Mark's gospel (1:21b-28). They give descriptions, noted the pope, of "four models of preaching: Jesus, the scribes, the priest Eli and behind him—they don't appear explicitly, but they are there—Eli's two sons, who are both priests."

The scribes taught and preached laying heavy burdens on people's shoulders. "And the poor folk couldn't carry them," said the pope. Jesus rebuked them because they didn't lift a finger to help these people. And later he told the people: "Do what they tell you but not what they do." They were inconsistent, explained the pope, speaking of the scribes and Pharisees, who behaved as if they were "beating people up." And Jesus warned them, "telling them: by doing that you close the doors of heaven; you don't let anyone in and you don't enter either."

It's the same today, insisted the pope. Some still use this wrong model of preaching, teaching, bearing witness to their faith. "And how many there are," he lamented, "who think the faith is like that."

Then the bishop of Rome turned to Eli's way of behaving, who was "an old man ... a poor old fellow," who, he confessed, "I feel rather sorry for," but who still "wasn't a really good man; he was a poor priest, who was weak and let things go, not really strong. He let his sons do so many bad things." The Holy Father told the story of Eli who mistook a poor woman for drunk because she was praying in silence, hardly moving her lips, asking the Lord to give her a child. She "prayed as humble folk pray, simply, from the heart, in distress; she moved her lips. So many good women pray like that in our churches and shrines. And this woman was praying like that, asking for a miracle. And Eli, the poor old fellow, would have nothing to do with it. He looked at her and thought: that woman's drunk. And he despised her. He was the representative of the faith," the one who should have taught the faith but "his heart wasn't right and he despised that woman. He told her, go away, you're drunk!"

"How often," said the Holy Father, "do the people of God feel they are disliked by those who should bear witness, by Christians, laity, priests, and bishops!" Then returning to Eli, Pope Francis explained why he felt a certain sympathy for him: "because he still had his anointing in his heart. When the woman explains her situation to him, Eli tells her: go in peace, may the God of Israel grant what you have asked. His priestly anointing comes out. Poor man, he'd hidden it under his idleness. He was lukewarm. And then he came to a bad end, poor fellow!"

In the Bible passage, observed the pope, his sons don't appear, but they were the ones who managed the temple. "They were crooks. They were priests," said the pope, "but crooks. They pursued power and money. They exploited the people; they profited from their alms and gifts. The Bible tells us that they took the best pieces of the sacrificial meat to eat for themselves. They were exploiters. The Lord punished them harshly, those two!"

For the pope they represent "the figure of the corrupt Christian, the corrupt lay person, the corrupt priest, the corrupt bishop. They take advantage of the situation, of the privilege of faith, of being Christians. And their hearts are corrupted. Think of Judas: perhaps he began to put his hand into the common purse for the first time out of jealousy or envy," and thus "his heart began to become corrupted. John, the good apostle who loves all the world, who preaches love, says of Judas: he was a thief. Period. It's clear:

he was corrupt. And from that corrupt heart came betrayal. He betrayed Jesus."

Finally, there's Jesus' own way of preaching. What's special about it? Why do the people say, "This man teaches as someone with authority; is this a new teaching?" Jesus, said the pope, "taught the law; he taught about Moses and the prophets. What was new about that? He has power, the power of holiness, because the unclean spirits go away. What's new about Jesus is that he brings God's word with him, God's message that is God's love for each of us. He brings God close to people. And to do so he also gets close himself. Close to sinners, he goes to dinner with Matthew, a thief, a traitor to his country; he forgives the adulterous woman, who the law said should be punished; he talks theology with the Samaritan woman, who was 'no angel'; she had her history." So Jesus "goes to the heart of each person, he gets close to each wounded heart. Jesus is interested only in the person and in God. And he tries to bring God close to each person and each person to God."

And again: "Jesus is like the good Samaritan, who cures life's wounds. Jesus is the intercessor who goes off alone to the mountain to pray for people, and gives his life for them. Jesus wants people to come to him and he seeks them; he feels moved when he sees them like sheep without a shepherd. And all this is what the people call a new attitude. No, it's not the teaching that's new, it's his way of making it new. The lucidity of the gospel."

"Let us ask the Lord," Pope Francis concluded, "that these two readings may help us in our Christian lives," so that in the part we have been called upon to play in the church's mission, each of us may not be merely legalistic, or even hypocritical like the scribes and Pharisees. "May we not be corrupt like Eli's sons; not lukewarm like Eli, but like Jesus, with that eagerness to seek people out, heal people, love people."

An Examination of Conscience

Thursday, January 16, 2014
1 Sam 4:1-11; Mk 1:40-45

"Are we ashamed of the scandals in the church?" Pope Francis proposed a deep examination of conscience this morning, Thursday, January 16, in his homily during the Mass celebrated at St. Martha's. An examination of conscience that gets to the root of the reasons for "so many" scandals, which he said he didn't want to mention individually, but that "we all know where they are."

And it's because of the scandals that "the holy people of God aren't given the bread of life" but "poisonous food." Scandals came, the pope went on to explain, because "God's word was rare in those men and women" who caused them, taking advantage of "their position of power and comfort in the church" but without having anything to do with "God's word." For, he made clear, it's worth nothing to say "I wear a medal" or "I wear a cross" if you don't have "a living relationship with God and God's word!" Besides, the pope went on, some of these scandals rightly meant "paying a great deal of money."

The pope's reflection was inspired by the prayer of the responsorial psalm—number 44 (43)—proclaimed in the day's liturgy, a prayer that refers to what was described in the first reading, Israel's defeat, in the first book of Samuel (4:1-11). The psalm quoted by the pope says: "Lord, you have rejected us and abased us, and have not gone out with our armies. You made us turn back from the foe, and our enemies have taken spoil for themselves." And these words, said the pope, "are the prayer of the just in Israel after all the many defeats it has suffered in its history."

Defeats that give rise to some questions: "Why did the Lord

leave Israel like that in the hands of the Philistines? Has the Lord forsaken his people? Has he hidden his face?" The fundamental question, said the pope, was "Why has the Lord forsaken his people in that battle against their enemies? But not just their enemies, enemies of the Lord!" Enemies who "hated God," who "were pagans."

"The key to finding the answer" to this decisive question, the pope said, lay in some verses from yesterday's liturgy: "The word of the Lord was rare in those days" (1 Samuel 3:1). "Among his people," he explained still referring to the biblical passage, the word of the Lord was so rare that the boy Samuel didn't understand who was calling him. Thus the people "lived without the word of the Lord. It had gone from them." The old priest Eli was "weak" and "his sons, mentioned twice here," were "corrupt: they terrified the people and beat them up." So "without God's word, without God's strength," there was room for "clericalism" and "clerical corruption."

In that situation, the pope continued, the people realize they are "far from God and say 'let's go and get the ark.'" But they bring "the ark into the camp" as if it were a magic object. So they had not intended to seek the Lord but "a thing that was magic." And with the ark "they feel secure."

For their part "the Philistines grasped the danger," especially when they heard "the echo of the shout" that greeted the arrival of the ark in Israel's camp, and they wondered what it meant. "They discovered," continued the pope, "that the ark of the Lord had arrived in Israel's camp." In fact we read in the book of Samuel: "The Philistines were afraid of it and said, 'God has come into the camp!'" So the Philistines thought they had gone to get God and that he had really come into their camp. But the people of Israel didn't realize that the ark "hadn't brought life" into the camp. Then the Bible tells us in detail about their two defeats by the Philistines: in the first one the deaths suffered were about four thousand; in the second, thirty thousand. And as well as that, "the ark of God was captured by the Philistines, and Eli's two sons, Hophni and Phinehas, died."

"This passage makes us ask," noted the pope, "how is our relationship with God, God's word? Is it a formal relationship; a distant relationship? Does God's word enter our hearts, change our hearts; has it that power or not?" Or "is it a formal relationship, sort of all right but with our hearts closed to that word?"

A series of questions, said the pope, that "lead us to think of the church's many defeats. So many defeats of the people of God." Defeats due "simply" to the fact that the people "don't hear the Lord, don't seek the Lord, don't let the Lord seek them." Then after the disaster has happened they turn to the Lord and ask, "But, Lord, what's happened?" In Psalm 44 (43) we read: "You have made us the taunt of our neighbors, the derision and scorn of those around us. You have made us a byword among the nations, a laughing stock among the peoples." And that leads us, noted Pope Francis, "to think of the church's scandals. But are we ashamed of them?" And he added: "So many scandals that I don't want to mention individually, but we all know about them. We know where they are!" Some "scandals," he said, "have meant paying a lot of money. That's all right…" And it was at this point that he spoke out without mincing his words about "the church's shame" because of these scandals, which sound like so many "defeats for priests, bishops, and laity."

The point is, the pope continued, that "the word of God in those scandals was rare. In those men, those women, the word of God was rare. They didn't have any bond with God. They had a position in the church, a position of power, and of comfort." But "not God's word." And "it's not worth anything to say 'but I wear a medal, I wear a cross': like those who brought the ark without a living relationship with God and God's word!" And recalling Jesus' words about scandals, he repeated that they had brought about "a decadence of the people of God, weakness, corruption of priests."

Pope Francis concluded his homily with two thoughts: God's word and God's people. Regarding the former, he suggested an examination of conscience: "Is the word of God alive in our hearts? Does it change our life or is it like the ark that comes and goes? Or "an evangeliary that's very beautiful," but which "doesn't reach our hearts?" As for the people of God, the pope dwelled on the harm that scandals do to them. "Poor people," he said, "poor people! We're not giving them the bread of life to eat! We're not giving them truth to eat! So often we're giving them poisonous food."

Così Fan Tutti: What Everyone Does

Friday, January 17, 2014
1 Sam 8:4-7, 10-22a; Mk 2:1-12

"Spiritual worldliness" is a dangerous temptation because it "makes the heart impressionable" with selfishness and gives Christians "an inferiority complex," which leads them to conform to the world, to do "what everyone does," following "the most agreeable fashion." At the Mass celebrated on Friday, January 17, in the chapel of St. Martha's House, Pope Francis spoke about "spiritual heedfulness" without "selling" our own identity.

As he has done recently, for his reflection the pope took his cue from the liturgical reading, a passage from the book of Samuel. "We've seen," he explained, "how the people had strayed far from God. They had lost the knowledge of God's word: they didn't hear it, they didn't meditate on it." And when "the word of God isn't there," he said, "its place is taken by another word: our own word, the word of our own selfishness, our own will. And also the world's word."

Meditating on the book of Samuel, "we have seen," he continued, "how the people, far from God's word, had suffered those defeats," which caused so many deaths and left behind "widows and orphans." They were "the defeats" of a people that "had strayed far" from the way pointed out to them by the Lord.

Straying far from God, noted the pope, means taking a road that inevitably "leads to what we heard in the reading today (1 Samuel 8:4-7, 10-22a): the people reject God. Not only do they fail to hear God's word, but they reject him" and end up saying: "We can rule ourselves, we're free and we want to go that way."

Samuel, the pope continued, "is distressed by this and goes to the Lord. And the Lord, with the good sense he has," suggests to Samuel: "Listen to the voice of the people in all that they say to you; for they have not rejected you but they have rejected me from being king over them."

Basically, the pope explained, "the Lord lets the people continue to distance themselves from him," making them "experience" what that distance means. "And Samuel," the pope went on to say, "tries to convince them, tells them all the things we heard in the reading, what the king will do to them and to their sons and their daughters." However, despite these warnings, "the people refuse to listen to Samuel's voice" and ask to have "a king as a governor."

And here, explained the pope, we have the decisive "saying," "the key" to understanding the matter. In fact, the people answer Samuel: "We will be like other nations." That's their first thought, "the first proposal: a king to 'govern us' like all the other nations."

A request, declared the pope, motivated by one fact: they had "forgotten that they were a chosen people. The Lord's people. A people chosen with love, led by the hand" of God, as "a father carries a child." They "forgot all that love" and wanted to become like all the other nations.

That wish, said the pope, "will constantly return as a temptation in the history of the chosen people. Remember the time of the Maccabees, when they traded being a chosen people for becoming like all the other nations. It's a real rebellion. The people rebel against the Lord." And that, he pointed out, "was opening the door to worldliness: doing what everyone does. With the values we have but doing what others do" and not "what you who have chosen me tell me to do." The practical consequence is that "they reject the Lord of love, they reject their chosen status. And they follow the way of the world."

Of course, said the pope, "it's true that Christians should be normal, like other normal people. That was already said in the Letter to Diogenetus, in early church times. But," he warned, "there are values that Christians can't accept." In fact, "they must keep God's word which tells them: you are my children, you are chosen; I am with you, I walk with you." And "normal life requires Christians to be faithful to their having been chosen." They must never "sell out for the sake of worldly conformity; that's the people's temptation and also our own."

Pope Francis warned against the temptation of forgetting "God's word, what the Lord tells us," in order to follow "the word of fashion." And he commented: "Even what a soap opera says can be the fashion: 'Let's go by that: it's more amusing!'" This "worldly" attitude, he declared, "is more dangerous because it's subtler," while "apostasy," that is, "the actual sin of breaking away from the Lord," is seen and clearly recognized.

Besides, saying that "we will be like all the other nations" shows that the people "were feeling a certain inferiority complex because they weren't a normal nation. And the temptation's there to say: we know what we ought to do; let the Lord stay quietly at home!" That, basically, was what they thought, which isn't that far from "the story of the first sin," the temptation to go our own way and to discern for ourselves how to "know good and evil."

"Temptation," the pope declared, "hardens the heart. And

when the heart is hard, when the heart isn't open, God's word can't enter it." It was no accident that Jesus said "to those on the road to Emmaus: you foolish and slow of heart!" because "their hearts were hardened; they couldn't understand God's word."

"Worldliness makes the heart impressionable." But that can "harm" it. Because, noted the pope, "it's never a good thing to have a heart that's too impressionable. What's good is a heart that's open to God's word and welcomes it. Like Mary, who pondered all these things in her heart, says the gospel." And so the priority is: "Welcome God's word so as not to stray far from our election."

"In the prayer at the beginning of Mass," the pope recalled, "we asked for the grace to overcome our selfishness," especially, wanting to do our own will. Pope Francis suggested, in conclusion, that we should renew our request to the Lord for this grace. And also ask for "the grace of spiritual heedfulness, to open our hearts to God's word," so as "not to do what those people did, who closed their hearts because they had strayed far from God and hadn't heard or understood God's word for a long time." "May the Lord give us the grace," he prayed, "of an open heart to welcome God's word," "meditate on it always," and "go the right way."

The God of Surprises

Monday, January 20, 2014
1 Sam 15:16-23; Mk 2:18-22

Discernment and heedfulness: two words that describe the right attitude to live in the freedom of God's word, breaking routines and habits and being able to adapt to continual surprises and newness. That was the reflection offered by Pope Francis in the Mass celebrated on Monday morning, January 20, in the chapel of St. Martha's House.

As usual, the pope focused his meditation on the day's liturgical readings, taken from the first book of Samuel (15:16-23) and from Mark's gospel (2:18-22), which help us "reflect on God's word" and on "our attitude to God's word." And God's word is "living and active; it discerns the thoughts and intentions of the heart," explained the pope, quoting from the letter to the Hebrews (4:12-13). In fact, "God's word comes to us and throws light upon the state of our heart, our soul"; in a word, it "discerns."

Both readings, he said, "tell us about this attitude we should have" toward "God's word: heedfulness." It's a matter of "heeding God's word. God's word is alive. And so it comes and tells us what it wants to say, not what I'm expecting or what I hope it will say or want it to say." God's word "is free." And "it also surprises, because our God is a God of surprises; he always comes and does something new. He is newness. The gospel is newness. Revelation is newness."

"Our God," continued the pope, "is a God who always makes things new. And he asks us to welcome his newness." In the gospel passage "Jesus is clear about this, he's very clear: new wine in new wineskins." So "God must be received with that openness to what is new." And that attitude "is called heedfulness."

Hence the invitation to ask ourselves some questions: "Do I heed God's word or do I always do what I believe is God's word? Or do I distill God's word so that in the end it becomes something other than what God wants?" But, the pope warned, "if I do that, I end up like the piece of new unshrunk cloth used to patch an old garment," about which the gospel speaks, "and the rip becomes worse; if I try to patch it that way it becomes worse."

So "adapting to God's word in order to be able to receive it" requires "an ascetic attitude," the pope explained, giving a practical example: "if the electric appliance I have doesn't work," I need "an adapter." And we must do the same with ourselves: "always adapt, adapt to this newness of God's word." Basically, "be open to newness."

The pope then turned in his reflection to the passage from the first book of Samuel. "Saul, chosen by God, anointed by God, had forgotten," the pope noted, "that God is surprise and newness. He'd forgotten. He'd shut himself off within his own ideas, his own plans. Thus he reasoned in a human way. The Lord had told him: Destroy them all." But "it was the habit when a battle was won," explained the pope, "to take booty" to divide it up; "and with part of the loot sacrifice was offered" to God. So Samuel had reserved some fine animals for the Lord: "He'd reasoned with his thoughts, his heart, which were bound by habit. And God, our God, isn't a God of habits; he's a God of surprises."

So "Saul didn't obey God's word." We read in the Bible that Samuel "rebuked him for this," saying: "Has the Lord as great delight in burnt offerings and sacrifices, as in obedience to the voice of the Lord?" Thus Samuel "makes him feel he hasn't obeyed: he wasn't a servant, he was the master. He made himself master of God's word. Samuel then says: 'To obey is better than sacrifice, and to heed than the fat of rams.'"

And then, continued the pope, "God's word goes further, by means of Samuel. The rebellion—not obeying God's word—'is the sin of divination,' the sin of magic. And stubbornness, heedlessness—doing what you want and not what God wants—is the sin of idolatry."

Samuel's words "make us think about what Christian freedom means, what Christian obedience mean," said the pope. "Christian freedom and Christian obedience mean heeding God's word; having the courage to become new wineskins for this new wine, which keeps coming. The courage always to discern, discern—not moderate—what the spirit is doing in my heart, what the spirit in my heart wants, where the spirit in my heart is leading me. And obey." He concluded with the two key words of his meditation, "discern and obey," and with a prayer: "Let us ask today for the grace of receptivity to God's word, to that word that is living and active, which discerns the intentions and thoughts of the heart."

God Chooses the Little Ones

Tuesday, January 21, 2014
1 Sam 16:1-13a; Mk 2:23-28

God always chooses "the littlest." He calls them by name and becomes involved in a personal relationship with them: that's why conversing with him means we must first of all become "little." Pope Francis reminded us of this during the Mass celebrated in the chapel of St. Martha's House on Tuesday morning, January 21, on the feast day of St. Agnes virgin and martyr.

The reflection for his homily was suggested by the reading from the first book of Samuel (16:1-13a), which relates the anointing of David. "The Lord's relationship with his people," he said, "is a personal relationship, always." A "person-to-person relationship: the Lord's people and the Lord, and the people have a name. Every person has a name. It's not a conversation between a great one and the masses," but a "personal" conversation. Besides, continued the pope, "persons are organized as a people or nation and the conversation is with this people, in which each person has a place."

And for that reason, he explained, "the Lord never speaks to us in general," as if to the "masses." Rather "he always speaks personally," to each person by name. Besides, the Lord "chooses personally," added the pope, suggesting the example of the "creation story. The same Lord who creates man with his own hands like a potter, gives him a name: I call you Adam. And that's how the relationship between God and the human person begins."

Pope Francis then pointed out another fundamental aspect: "It's a relationship between God and us little ones. God is great and we are little." So "when God has to choose a person, and also his people, he always chooses the little ones." So much so that "he tells his people: I chose you because you were the littlest, the one who has the least power among the nations."

So there's the basic reason for the "conversation between God and human littleness." Here the pope referred to the witness of "Mary, who will say: the Lord has looked upon my lowliness; he has looked upon those who are little, he has chosen the little ones."

"And in today's first reading," continued the pope, "we clearly see this attitude of the Lord. When Samuel stands before the tallest of Jesse's sons, he says: 'Surely the Lord's anointed is now before the Lord!' Because he was a big, tall man." But the Lord, added the pope, says to Samuel: "Do not look on his appearance or on the height of his stature, because I have rejected him; for the Lord does not see as mortals see: they look on the outward appearance, but the Lord looks on the heart."

So "the Lord chooses according to his own criteria." That's why, the pope declared, "in the prayer at the beginning of Mass, looking at St. Agnes, we prayed: You, Lord, who choose what is weak and humble to confound the strong of the earth…"

Referring again to the Bible reading, the Holy Father reiterated that "the Lord chooses David, the littlest, who for his father didn't count. His father thought he wasn't at home, and perhaps he'd told him: go and look after the sheep because we have to settle an important affair here and you don't count." Whereas it was David, the littlest, who "was chosen" by the Lord and anointed by Samuel.

"All of us have been chosen by the Lord through baptism. We've all been chosen," said the pope, explaining that the Lord "chose us one by one. He gave us a name. And he watches us. It's a conversation. For that's how the Lord loves us."

But even David, when he became king, "made mistakes" and "perhaps he made many mistakes." The Bible tells us of "two big ones, two grave mistakes." And "what did David do? He humbled himself; he returned to his littleness and said: I'm a sinner. He asked for forgiveness and did penance."

Thus "after his second sin, when he'd wanted to see how strong his people was, the Lord made him see that the census was an act of pride." And David "said: but punish me and not the people! The people are not to blame; I'm the guilty one!" By doing this "David kept his littleness: through repentance and through prayer." And also by weeping, because "when he was fleeing from his enemies, he wept. And he said to himself: perhaps the Lord will see this weeping and have pity on us!"

Continuing with his reflection on "this conversation between the Lord and our littleness, the littleness of each of us," the pope asked a question: "Where does Christian faithfulness lie?" And he answered: "Christian faithfulness, our faithfulness, simply means holding on to our littleness so that it can converse with the Lord." That's why "humility, mildness, gentleness are so important in Christian life: they are the way we hold on to our littleness." They are the bases upon which to carry on "the conversation between our littleness and the Lord's greatness."

Pope Francis concluded his homily with a prayer: "May the Lord grant us, through the intercession of Mary—who sang joyfully to God because he had looked upon her lowliness—the grace to hold on to our littleness in his sight."

Hearts Free from Envy and Jealousy

Thursday, January 23, 2014
1 Sam 18:6-9, 19:1-7; Mk 3:7-12

With a prayer that "the seed of jealousy may not be sown" in Christian communities and envy not dwell in the hearts of believers, Pope Francis concluded his homily at the Mass celebrated this morning, Thursday, January 23, at St. Martha's.

The pope's whole reflection focused on the subject of jealousy and envy, which he described as the gates through which the devil entered the world. The bishop of Rome took his cue from the first reading, the first book of Samuel (18:6-9; 19:1-7), which tells how, after God's people's victory over the Philistines, won mainly thanks to the courage of David, the women came out from all Israel's cities to meet King Saul with singing and dancing. And he too, commented he pope, "was happy, but he also heard something he didn't like. When the women praised David because he had killed the Philistine," something filled the king's heart with "bitterness and distress." And hearing the women's singing, he was "very angry"; the words they were singing "sounded all wrong."

And it was at that very moment, the Holy Father noted, that "a great victory began to become a defeat in the king's heart. He became bitter." That reminds us of "what took place in Cain's heart: the worm of jealousy and envy entered it." The same thing happened to Saul as had happened to Cain when the Lord asked him: "But why are you resentful? Why are you walking with your head down?" In fact, explained Pope Francis, "the worm of jealousy brings resentment, envy, bitterness" and also leads to instinctive actions, like killing someone. It's not by accident that Saul fosters the same determination as Cain: to kill. He decides to kill David.

"The same thing still happens today," added the pope, "in our hearts. It's an ugly distress that won't tolerate a brother or sister having something I haven't got." And so "instead of praising God, as the women did for Israel's victory," Saul prefers to shut himself off, "to become resentful, simmer, and seethe with bitterness."

Besides, jealousy and envy are the gates through which the devil entered the world, continued the pope, stressing that the Bible tells us so: "Through the devil's envy evil came into the world." And "jealousy and envy open the gates to all evil things," and end up creating rifts even between believers. The pope referred explicitly to the life of Christian communities, stressing that "when some members suffer from jealousy and envy, they end up divided." Divisions that Pope Francis called "a strong poison," the same as what we find at the beginning of the Bible with Cain.

The Holy Father then described what actually happens "in the heart of a person who feels this jealousy, this envy." There are two main consequences. The first is bitterness: "The envious and jealous person is a bitter person, who can't sing or praise, feels no joy, is always looking out for" what others have. And sadly, that bitterness "spreads right through the community," because all those who fall victims to that poison become "spreaders of bitterness."

The second consequence is gossip. Someone can't bear another person having something, explained the pope, and so "the solution is to put that person down, to vaunt myself. And the way to do so is gossip; if you look you'll see that behind gossip there's always jealousy and envy."

So "gossip divides the community, destroys the community: it's the devil's weapon. How many fine Christian communities," the pope said sadly, "have we seen who were going well," but then into some of their members "the worm of jealousy and envy enters, bringing unhappiness with it," and their "hearts become resentful." So that's why we shouldn't forget the episode of Saul, because "after a great victory, a process of defeat begins. A person who is under the influence of envy and jealousy kills. Besides, "John the apostle told us: anyone who hates their brother is a murderer. And the envious and the jealous begin to hate their brothers."

So the Holy Father's final wish was: "Today at this Mass, let us pray for our Christian communities, that this seed of jealousy may not be sown among us. That envy may not take root in our heart or in the heart of our communities. And thus we can carry on praising the Lord, praising the Lord with joy." And, he concluded, let us pray "for a great grace: the grace not to fall into misery, resentment, jealousy, and envy."

How to Create Dialogue

Friday, January 24, 2014
1 Sam 24:3-21; Mk 3:13-19

Dialogue is created by humility, and at the cost of "swallowing many bitter pills," because we must not allow "walls" of resentment and hatred to rise in our hearts. This is what Pope Francis said at the Mass celebrated on Friday morning, January 24, on the feast of St. Francis of Sales, in the chapel of St. Martha's House.

The cue for his homily was the passage from the first book of Samuel (24:3-21), which tells the story of the confrontation between Saul and David. "Yesterday," recalled the pope, "we heard God's word," which "showed us what jealousy can do, what envy can do in families, in Christian communities." These are negative attitudes, which "always lead to so many quarrels, so many divisions. And also to hatred." And "we saw that happening in Saul's heart against David: he felt that jealousy," to the point where "he wanted to kill him."

But "today," he continued, "God's word shows us another attitude: that of David." David "knew quite well" that he was "in danger; he knew the king wanted to kill him. And he found himself in a situation where he could have killed the king. That would have been the end of the story." However, "he chose a different way." He preferred "the way of approaching, clarifying the situation, explaining himself—the way of dialogue in order to make peace."

But King Saul was "ruminating bitterness in his heart." He insulted "David because he thought he was his enemy. And that feeling grew in his heart." Unfortunately, said the pope, "these fantasies always grow when we listen to them within ourselves. And they build a wall which separates us from the other person." So we end up remaining "marooned in the bitter brew of our resentment."

Then David "by the Lord's inspiration" breaks that mechanism of hatred "and says: no, I want to talk with you!" And that's how "the way of peace begins," the pope explained, "with dialogue." But, he warned, "dialogue isn't easy, it's difficult." Nevertheless, it's only "by dialogue that we build bridges in a relationship, rather than walls that separate us."

"For dialogue," he made clear, "the first thing necessary is humility." We see that from the example of "David, who was humble, who said to the king: Look, I could have killed you, I could have done that, but I don't want to! I want to stay with you because you are the authority, you are the Lord's anointed!" What David did was "an act of humility."

So, for dialogue you don't need to raise your voice but "you do need gentleness." And then "it's necessary to realize that the other person has something more than me," as David did. Looking at Saul he said to himself: "He's the Lord's anointed; he's more important than me." As well as "humility and gentleness, what's needed for dialogue," added the pope, "is doing what we asked for yesterday in the prayer at the beginning of Mass: become all things to all people."

"Humility, gentleness, becoming all things to all people" are the three basic requirements for dialogue. But, the Holy Father pointed out, even though "it's not written in the Bible, we all know that doing these things means swallowing many bitter pills. We have to, because that's the way to make peace!" Peace is made "by humility, humiliation," always trying "to see God's image in the other person." In that way so many problems are solved "by dialogue in the family and in the community, in the neighborhood." We have to be prepared to admit to the other person: "But look, sorry, I thought that…" The right attitude is to "humble ourselves, always build bridges, always, always!" That's the style for anyone who wants "to be Christian"; even if, the pope admitted, "it's not easy. It's not easy!" And yet "Jesus did it: he humbled himself to the end, he showed us the way."

The pope then suggested another piece of practical advice: to open a dialogue "it's necessary that not too much time should pass." In fact, problems should be faced "as soon as possible, at the first moment they can be after the storm passes." We need immediately "to approach dialogue, because delay makes the wall grow higher," like "weeds shooting up that stop the wheat from growing." And he warned, "when walls go up reconciliation is so difficult; it's so difficult!" The bishop of Rome referred to the Berlin Wall, which separated people over so many years. And he said it's also possible to become like Berlin "in our hearts," with a wall standing between us and others. Hence his invitation "not to let too much time pass" and to "seek for peace as soon as possible."

In particular, the pope mentioned married couples. "It's normal to quarrel, it's normal." And seeing the smiles of some couples present, he repeated: "In marriage you quarrel, sometimes even plates are thrown." But, he advised, "never end the day without making peace, without a conversation; sometimes it can just be a gesture," making an appointment "for tomorrow."

"I'm afraid of these walls," said the pope, "that go up every day and foster resentments and also hatred." And he pointed again to the choice "made by young David: he could easily have avenged himself"; he could have killed the king, but "he chose the way of dialogue with humility, gentleness, and sweetness." And to conclude he asked "St. Francis of Sales, the doctor of sweetness," to give "all of us the grace to make bridges with others, never to build walls."

When Priests Don't Make News

Monday, January 27, 2014
2 Sam 5:1-7, 10; Mk 3:22-30

They don't make news in the papers but they give people strength and hope: these are all the "anonymous" bishops and priests who continue to offer their lives in Christ's name in the service of their diocese or parish. Pope Francis invited us to pray for these "brave, holy, good, faithful" priests during the Mass celebrated on Monday morning, January 27, in the chapel of St. Martha's House.

The pope's reflection took its cue from the first reading, the second book of Samuel (5:1-7, 10), which tells the story of David's anointing. "We heard the story of that meeting," he said. It was at Hebron when "all the tribes of Israel came to David and wanted to make him king." In fact, he explained, "David was king of Judah but the kingdom was divided." All the elders of the people "had seen that the only one who could" be king "was David." So "they went to him to make a covenant." And, the pope continued, "they must have talked it over, discussed how to make the covenant. And in the end they decided to make him king." But "that decision wasn't, let's say, democratic"; rather it was a unanimous acclaim: "you are king!"

And "this," the pope explained, "is the first step. Then comes the second: King David made a covenant with them," and the elders of the people "anointed David king of Israel." So that's the importance of anointing. "Without this anointing," he said, "David would have been just the boss, the manager of a company running this political society, the kingdom of Israel." Whereas "anointing is something else"; and it's "the anointing that consecrates David as king."

"What's the difference," the pope asked, "between being a political manager of a country and an anointed king?" He explained that when David "was anointed king of Judah by Samuel, he was a young boy. The Bible tells us that after the anointing the Spirit of the Lord fell upon David." So "anointing makes the Spirit of the Lord come down upon the person and be with them."

The passage read in the liturgy, noted the pope, "says the same: David became greater and greater, for the Lord, the God of hosts, was with him." And "that's what's special about anointing."

The bishop of Rome recalled David's attitude when he confronted King Saul, "who wanted to kill him out of jealousy and envy." David "had the opportunity to kill King Saul, but he didn't want to: I will never touch the Lord's anointed; he's a person chosen by the Lord, anointed by the Lord!" In his words there was "the sense of a king's sacredness."

"In the church," said the pope, "we've inherited that in the person of bishops and priests." In fact bishops "aren't chosen only to run an organization that is a particular church. They're anointed. They have received anointing and the spirit of the Lord is with them." All we priests, the pope made clear, "are sinners, all of us! But we're anointed!" And "we all want to become holier every day, more faithful to that anointing." And "what makes the church, what gives the church unity, is the person of the bishop, in the name of Jesus Christ, because of the anointing: not because he has been voted in by a majority but because he's been anointed."

"In that anointing lies the strength of a particular church, and its priests also share in the anointing: the bishop lays hands on them and brings the anointing upon them." So, said the pope, priests "look after parishes and do so much other work." It's their anointing that brings bishops close to the Lord; they are "chosen by the Lord." Thus "for bishops and priests that anointing is their strength and their joy." Their strength, he said, because it's in their anointing that they "find the calling to carry people forward, to help them." And also their joy "because they feel chosen by the Lord, protected by the Lord, by that love with which the Lord protects us all."

That's why, Pope Francis declared, "when we think of bishops and priests—both are priests because that's Christ's priesthood: bishop and priest—we must think like that: anointed." Otherwise, he made clear, "the church can't be understood." And "not only can it not be understood; but it can't be explained how the church carries on with only human strength." A "diocese carries on because it has a holy people, so many things, and it also has an anointed one who carries it forward, helps it to grow." The same goes for a parish, which "carries on because it has so many organizations, so many things, but also because it has a priest: an anointed one to carry it forward."

We only remember, the pope stressed, "a very few of so many holy bishops, so many priests, so many holy priests," who have given "their whole life in service of the diocese, the parish." And we may forget "how many people have found the power of faith, the power of love and hope from these anonymous parish priests, whom we don't know about. And there are so many!" They are "country priests or city priests, who through their anointing have given the people strength, have passed on doctrine, have given the sacraments, that is to say, holiness."

Someone might object, the pope noted: "But Father, I've read in the newspaper that a bishop has done such and such or a priest has done such and such!" An objection to which the pope replied: "Yes, so have I! But tell me, do the newspapers report news of what so many priests do, so many priests in so many parishes, city and country parishes? All the good they do? All the work they do to carry their people forward?" And he added: "No, that's not news!" The well-known proverb is right, he said: "One tree that falls makes more noise than a whole forest growing."

Pope Francis concluded his reflection by inviting us to think "of David's anointing" and therefore "of our brave, holy, good, faithful bishops and priests." And he asked us to pray "for them: thanks to them we are here today; they were the ones who baptized us."

THE PRAYER OF PRAISE

Tuesday, January 28, 2014
2 SAM 6:12B-15, 17-19; MK 3:31-35

It's hard to justify someone who feels ashamed to sing the Lord's praises, but then shouts his head off when his favorite team makes a goal. That was the point of Pope Francis' reflection on the morning of Tuesday, January 28, in his homily during the Mass celebrated in St. Martha's chapel.

Pope Francis pondered the description of the festival organized by David for the re-entry of the ark of the covenant, in the first reading of the day's liturgy (2 Samuel 6:12-15, 17-19). King David, recalled the pope, "offered sacrifices in God's honor;

he prayed. Then his prayer became exultant… it was a prayer of praise, of joy. And he began to dance. The Bible tells us: 'David danced before the Lord with all his might.'" And David was so happy in that prayer of praise that he "lost all composure" and began "to dance before the Lord, but with all his might." That, the pope insisted, was "really a prayer of praise."

Considering that episode, the bishop of Rome confided, "I immediately thought about the words of Sarah after she'd given birth to Isaac: 'The Lord has made me dance with joy.' That old woman of ninety danced for joy." David was young, he repeated, but he too "danced, danced before the Lord. That's an example of a prayer of praise."

Which is something different from the prayer we usually pray, the pope continued, "to ask the Lord for something" or also just "to thank the Lord," and neither is it difficult to understand the meaning of a prayer of worship. But, the Holy Father noted, "We leave out the prayer of praise." It's not a spontaneous thing for us. Some people, he added, might think it was a prayer "more suited to those in the renewal movement, not all Christians. But the prayer of praise is a Christian prayer for all of us. At Mass, every day, when we sing 'Holy, holy…,' that's a prayer of praise; we're praising God for his greatness because he is great. And we tell him beautiful things, because we're glad he's like that." And it doesn't matter whether we're good singers. In fact, explained Pope Francis, it's not possible to think "you're quite capable of shouting when your team gets a goal and not capable of singing praises to the Lord, losing your inhibitions and singing out."

Praising God "is completely gratuitous," he continued. "We aren't asking or thanking. We're praising: you are great. 'Glory be to the Father, the Son, and the Holy Spirit…' We say that with our whole heart. It's also right that we do, because he is great, he's our God. Think of a good question we can ask ourselves today: 'What's my prayer of praise like? Can I praise the Lord?

Or when I pray the Gloria or the Sanctus do I do so only with my lips and not with my whole heart? What does David dancing tell me? And Sarah dancing for joy?' When David enters the city, something else begins: the festival. The joy of praise leads us to the joy of the festival." A festival that then spreads to the family, "everyone," the pope pictured them, "at home feasting and partying."

However, when David returns to the palace, he's faced with the rebuke and scorn of Saul's daughter Michal: "'But aren't you ashamed to do what you've done? How can you do that, you the king, dancing in front of everybody? Aren't you ashamed?' I wonder how often in our hearts we despise good people who praise the Lord" like that spontaneously, just as it occurs to them, without any formality. But in the Bible, the pope recalled, we read that "Michal remained barren all her life for that. What does God's word mean here? That joy, the prayer of praise, makes us fruitful. Sarah dances at the great moment of her giving birth at the age of ninety! Fruitfulness gives praise to the Lord." Men and women who praise the Lord, who pray by praising the Lord—and when they do are happy to say so—and rejoice "when they sing the Sanctus at Mass," are fruitful people. But, added the pope, those who "shut themselves up in the formality of a cold, measured prayer end up like Michal, in the barrenness of their formality. Let us imagine David dancing with all his might before the Lord. Let us think how beautiful it is to offer prayers of praise. Perhaps it will do us good to repeat the words of the psalm we prayed today, Psalm 24 (23): 'Lift up your heads, O gates! And be lifted up, O ancient doors! that the king of glory may come in. The Lord, strong and mighty, he is the king of glory. Lift up your heads, O gates! Who is this king of glory? It's the Lord of hosts, the Lord of victory.'" That should be our prayer of praise, and, he concluded, when we raise it to the Lord, we should "say in our heart: 'Lift, heart, because you stand before the king of glory.'"

No Split Between Christ and the Church

Thursday, January 30, 2014
2 Sam 7:18-19, 24-29; Mk 4:21-25

The sensus ecclesiae—which saves us from "the absurd split of being Christians without the church"—rests on three pillars: humility, faithfulness, and the service of prayer. This is what Pope Francis said during the Mass celebrated on Thursday morning, January 30, in the chapel of St. Martha's House.

His reflection was suggested by the reading of Psalm 132 (131), which, the pope said, "opens the door for us to reflect on God's word in today's liturgy." He recited the text: "O Lord, remember in David's favor all the hardships he endured." So, explained the pope, here we have "King David as a model; King David as the man who has worked so hard, endured so many hardships for the kingdom of God."

A thought that links with "the passage from the second book of Samuel (7:18-19, 24-29), which we heard today, following on from yesterday," noted the Holy Father. The passage relates the thoughts of "David, who was so concerned about the Lord," that he worried: "I live in a palace but the ark of the Lord is still in a tent; let us build a temple." But the Lord replies in the negative: "No, you won't; your son will build it!" And "David accepts that, accepts with joy," presenting himself before God "like a son to a father."

David begins thus: "Who am I, Lord God, and what is my house, that you have brought me thus far?" First of all, remarked the pope, he asks himself: "Who am I?" He well remembers that he'd been "a young shepherd, as it says in another passage, who'd been taken from the sheep" to become "now king of Israel." So that's what David means by asking: "Who am I?"

A question, said the pope, which shows that "David had a

strong sense of belonging to the people of God." And that, he said, "made me reflect: it would be good to ask ourselves today what is the sign of our belonging to the church: feeling with the church, feeling in the church." Actually, he continued, "a Christian isn't someone who's been baptized, who receives baptism and then goes his own way." It's not like that, because "the first result of baptism is to make you belong to the church, to the people of God." So, he made clear, "you can't have a Christian without the church. That's why the great Paul VI said that it was an absurd split to love Christ without the church; listen to Christ and not the church; be with Christ apart from the church. It's an absurd split."

In fact, added Pope Francis, "we receive the gospel message in the church and we forge our holiness in the church. Our way is in the church." The alternative, he said, "is a fantasy" or, as Paul VI said, "an absurd split."

The pope then went more deeply into the meaning "of this feeling with the church. In Latin it's called sensus ecclesiae: it means feeling and thinking and willing within the church." And "reflecting on this passage about David, about his belonging to the people of God, we can find three pillars to support this belonging, this feeling with the church": humility, faithfulness, and the service of prayer.

As for the first pillar, the bishop of Rome explained, "someone who isn't humble can't feel with the church; they will feel what they like." True humility "can be seen in David," who asks: "Who am I, Lord God, and what is my house?" David "realizes that salvation history didn't begin with me and won't end when I die. No! It's a salvation history," by means of which "the Lord takes you, makes you walk on and then calls you; and the story goes on." So humility means being aware that "the history of the church began before us and will go on after us." For "we're a small part of a great people who walk the way of the Lord."

The second pillar, faithfulness, "is linked to obedience." Pope Francis pointed again to the figure of David, who "obeys the Lord and is also faithful to his teaching, his law." So "faithfulness to the church, faithfulness to her teaching, faithfulness to the Creed, faithfulness to her doctrine, and keeping that doctrine." Thus "humility and faithfulness" go together. "Paul VI also reminded us," said the pope, "that we receive the gospel message as a gift. But not as something we own. It's a gift we have received and which we give." And "in passing it on," we have to "be faithful, because we have received it and we have to give a gospel that isn't ours; it belongs to Jesus. We mustn't become owners of the gospel we received and use it as we like."

With humility and faithfulness, "the third pillar is service: service in the church. Service to God, service to our neighbor, our brothers and sisters," explained the Holy Father, "but here I will only mention service to God." The starting point is still David's attitude: when "he finishes offering his thoughts to God, which is a prayer, he prays for the people of God." For "that's the third pillar: praying for the church."

We read in this passage from the Old Testament: "O Lord God, you are God and your words are true, and you have promised this good thing to your servant." And, commented the pope, the Lord has also assured us that "the church won't be destroyed" and the gates of hell will not prevail "against her." The passage from the second book of Samuel continues thus: "And now therefore may it please you to bless the house of your servant, so that it may continue forever before you!" These words suggest a question: "How is our prayer for the church? Do we pray for the church? At Mass, every day, but at home, do we? Do we when we say our prayers?" We must pray to the Lord for "the whole church everywhere in the world." That's the essence of "service in God's sight that is prayer for the church."

So, the pope summarized, humility makes us understand that

"we belong to a community as a great grace" and that "salvation history doesn't begin with me and won't end with me. Each one of us can say that." Faithfulness reminds us that "we have received a gospel, a doctrine," which we must be faithful to and keep. And service impels us to be constant in "prayer for the church." And in conclusion he prayed, "May the Lord help us to walk this way to deepen our belonging to the church and feeling with the church."

Martyrs Who Pay for Our Sins

Friday, January 31, 2014
2 Sam 11:1-4a, 5-10a, 13-17; Mk 4:26-34

There is a danger of becoming Christians who are "too secure," of losing "the sense of sin," of being seduced by "a worldly vision of being super-powerful" that makes you think you can do everything on your own. This was the gist of Pope Francis' homily during the Mass on Friday morning, January 31, in the chapel of St. Martha's House.

He referred to the biblical episode of David's temptation, when he became intoxicated with Bathsheba, the wife of his faithful soldier Uriah; so he took her for himself and sent her husband off to die in battle. The loss of the sense of sin, said the pope, is the sign of how the meaning of the kingdom of God withers away. It makes us forget how salvation comes from God "and not from human cleverness."

Taking his cue from the day's liturgy, the pope focused his homily on the kingdom of God. The passage from Mark (4:26-34), said the pope, "speaks to us about the kingdom of God," how it grows. In fact, we read in the gospel that "no one, not even the sower," knows how this happens. But in another passage, the

pope explained, Jesus tells us that it's God himself who makes his
kingdom grow in us. "And this growth," he said, "is a gift from
God we must ask for." And we ask for it every day when we say
"the Our Father: your kingdom come!" A prayer, he noted, that
"means: may your kingdom grow within us, in society. May the
kingdom of God grow!"

But "just as it can grow," he warned, "the kingdom of God
can also wither away." And "that's what the first reading is telling
us about." The reading, taken from the second book of Samuel
(11:1-4a, 5-10a, 13-17), relates the temptation of David. To explain the passage, Pope Francis referred back to the readings of
the day before, in particular to "David's beautiful prayer to the
Lord: his prayer for his people." It's "the king who prays for his
people; it's the prayer of a saint." But "the following year," said the
pope, "there comes what we've heard about today" in the second
book of Samuel: David's temptation. And it's what devastates
the kingdom, which for the most part had been peaceful, despite
small wars to control its frontiers. And also "David is peaceful";
he leads "a normal life." But one day "he's taking a siesta after
lunch; then he gets up and goes for a walk and is tempted. David
falls into temptation" when he sees Bathsheba, Uriah's wife.

"This is something that could happen to any of us," commented the pope, because "we're all sinners and we're all tempted.
Temptation is our daily bread." So much so, he noted, that "if
any of us said 'I've never been tempted,'" the right answer to that
would be: "You're either an angel or a bit stupid!" In fact, "it's
normal for us to struggle in life; the devil doesn't rest and wants
his victory."

Indeed, "the most serious problem in this passage," the pope
pointed out, "is not so much the temptation or the sin against the
ninth commandment. It's how David behaves." In fact, in this
situation he loses his awareness of sin and simply talks about "a
problem" to solve. And his attitude "is a sign" because "when the

kingdom of God withers away, one of the signs is that the sense of sin is lost." David, explained the pope, commits "a grave sin," but he "doesn't feel" that it is. For him it's just a "problem." So "it doesn't occur to him to ask for forgiveness." He is only concerned to solve the problem. After he has been with Bathsheba she becomes pregnant and David asks himself: "How can I cover up my adultery?"

So he adopts a strategy to make Uriah think the baby his wife is carrying is his. Uriah, explained the pope, "was a good Israelite: he thought about his comrades and didn't want to celebrate while the army of Israel was fighting." But after having tried in vain to persuade him "with wine and feasting," David "as a decisive man, a ruler, makes a decision" and writes a letter to Joab, the captain of the army, ordering him to send Uriah to the forefront of the battlefield, so that he will be killed. "And that's what happened. Uriah is killed. And he's killed because he was put where he was so that he would be killed": it was "murder."

Nevertheless, "when King David hears that this has happened, he remains calm and carries on with his life." And the reason? David "had lost his sense of sin and at that moment the kingdom of God began to drop away" below the horizon. This is shown by the fact that David doesn't "refer to God"; he doesn't say: "Lord, see what I've done; what shall we do?" Now he is overcome by "that vision of being all-powerful: I can do anything!" This is an attitude of "worldliness."

The same thing "can happen to us," said the pope, "when we lose the sense of the kingdom of God and, consequently, the sense of sin." And he recalled the words of Pius XII pointing out that "the evil of this civilization is that it has lost the sense of sin: feeling we can do anything, we can solve everything ourselves. Human power replacing the glory of God!"

That's a way of thinking, noted the pope, that has become "daily bread." Hence our "daily prayer to God: Your kingdom come! May your kingdom grow!" For "salvation won't come from our cleverness, our cunning, our intelligence in doing things." No, "salvation will come by the grace of God and by the daily training we receive from this grace"; that is "Christian living."

Pope Francis then listed the people named in the biblical passage: David, Bathsheba, Joab, but also "the courtiers" who were all around David and "knew everything: it was a true scandal but they weren't scandalized, because they too" had "lost the sense of sin." And then there's "poor Uriah who pays the price."

And it was Uriah who gave rise to the Holy Father's final reflection: "I confess to you that when I see these injustices, that human pride," or "when I become aware of the danger that I myself" might fall into, "of losing the sense of sin," he admitted, "I think it does us good to think about all those Uriahs in history, all those Uriahs today who also suffer from our Christian mediocrity." Mediocrity that prevails when "we lose the sense of sin and allow the kingdom of God to fall."

People like Uriah, he said, "are the unrecognized martyrs who pay for our sins." So, added the pope, "it will do us good to pray for ourselves today, that the Lord may always give us the grace not to lose the sense of sin and that the kingdom of God may not wither away in us." And he concluded by inviting us "to bring a spiritual flower to the tombs of those contemporary Uriahs, who pay the price for those who are secure, those Christians who feel secure. And who, with or without wanting to, commit murder."

MORNING HOMILIES

Pope Francis

"Since Pope Francis's election, I have read his beautiful morning homilies, and their publication is something I've long been anticipating ... I hope that his surprising insights will lead you deeper into Scripture and help you encounter God in a new way."
—*James Martin, S.J.*

Each morning when Pope Francis celebrates Mass he offers a short homily for fellow residents and guests in the chapel of St. Martha's Guesthouse, where he has chosen to live. Now, the first volume of Morning Homilies, which offers reflections from late March through July of 2013, and includes three talks at World Youth Day in Brazil, makes it possible for everyone to experience his lively interpretations of Scripture and his uncanny capacity to engage his listeners, capturing the tenor of daily life.

Francis reflects on the disciples on the road to Emmaus, "simmering their lives in the sauce of their grumbling;" urges Christians to face daily life "ready, like the goalkeeper of a football team, to stop the ball wherever it comes from"; and notes our habit of "going to confession like going to the dry cleaners" as well as the "holy picture face" which we put on to conceal our own sinfulness.

Even more important than these memorable images are the themes that arise again and again in the Pope's preaching: the importance of mercy and forgiveness; the role of Jesus as Savior; the dangers of a church closed in on itself; and the gospel as an unfailing source of life and joy.

224pp., scripture references, softcover.
ISBN 978-1-62698-111-9

ORBIS BOOKS
Maryknoll, New York 10545

From your bookseller or direct: www.orbisbooks.com
Call toll free 1-800-258-5838 M-F 8-4 ET

ALL SHALL BE WELL
Readings for Lent and Easter

MICHAEL LEACH, JAMES KEANE, DORIS GOODNOUGH,
EDITORS

A treasure of inspired and inspiring readings from cherished writers to enrich every day of the Lenten season, through Easter week—and beyond.

From the first day of Lent through Easter Sunday and beyond, these 54 readings from beloved writers, classical and contemporary, will surprise you with joy, touch you with love, and comfort you with peace. A wonderful book for daily inspiration during the Lenten season and to re-read for its beauty and wisdom on many days after. The authors include

James Martin, SJ
Joyce Rupp
Daniel Berrigan
Dorothy Day
Pope Francis
Joan Chittister
Henri Nouwen

Phyllis Tickle
John Updike
Carlo Carrettp
Brian Doyle
Pope St John XXIII
T.S. Eliot
Thomas Merton

and many more.

Michael Leach, editor-at-large for Orbis Books, has edited many anthologies, including *A Maryknoll Book of Inspiration* (Orbis) and the bestseller *I Like Being Catholic* (Doubleday/Image). James T. Keane is acquisitions editor at Orbis Books. Doris Goodnough is rights&permissions coordinator at Orbis Books. They have also co-editing *Goodness and Light: Readings for Advent and Christmas*.

280pp., index, 5 X 7 paperback
ISBN 978-1-62698-139-3

ORBIS BOOKS
Maryknoll, New York 10545

From your bookseller or direct: www.orbisbooks.com
Call toll free 1-800-258-5838 M-F 8-4 ET